DO YOU KNOW
Komodo Dragons?

Written by
Alain M. Bergeron
Michel Quintin
Sampar

Illustrations by
Sampar

Translated by
Solange Messier

Fitzhenry & Whiteside

First published as "Savais-Tu? Les Dragons de Komodo" by Editions Michel Quintin, Québec, Canada
Published in Canada by Fitzhenry & Whiteside, 195 Allstate Parkway, Markham, Ontario L3R 4T8

Published in the United States by Fitzhenry & Whiteside, 311 Washington Street, Brighton, Massachusetts 02135

www.fitzhenry.ca godwit@fitzhenry.ca

10 9 8 7 6 5 4 3 2 1

Library and Archives Canada Cataloguing in Publication
Do You Know Komodo Dragons?
ISBN 9781554553396 (pbk.)
Data available on file

Publisher Cataloging-in-Publication Data (U.S.)
Do You Know Komodo Dragons?
ISBN 9781554553396 (pbk.)
Data available on file

Fitzhenry & Whiteside acknowledges with thanks the Canada Council for the Arts, and the Ontario Arts Council for their support of our publishing program. We acknowledge the financial support of the Government of Canada through the Canada Book Fund (CBF) for our publishing activities.

Canada Council for the Arts
Conseil des Arts du Canada
ONTARIO ARTS COUNCIL
CONSEIL DES ARTS DE L'ONTARIO
50 YEARS OF ONTARIO GOVERNMENT SUPPORT OF THE ARTS
50 ANS DE SOUTIEN DU GOUVERNEMENT DE L'ONTARIO AUX ARTS

Cover and text design by Daniel Choi
Cover image by Sampar
Printed in China by Sheck Wah Tong Printing Press Ltd.

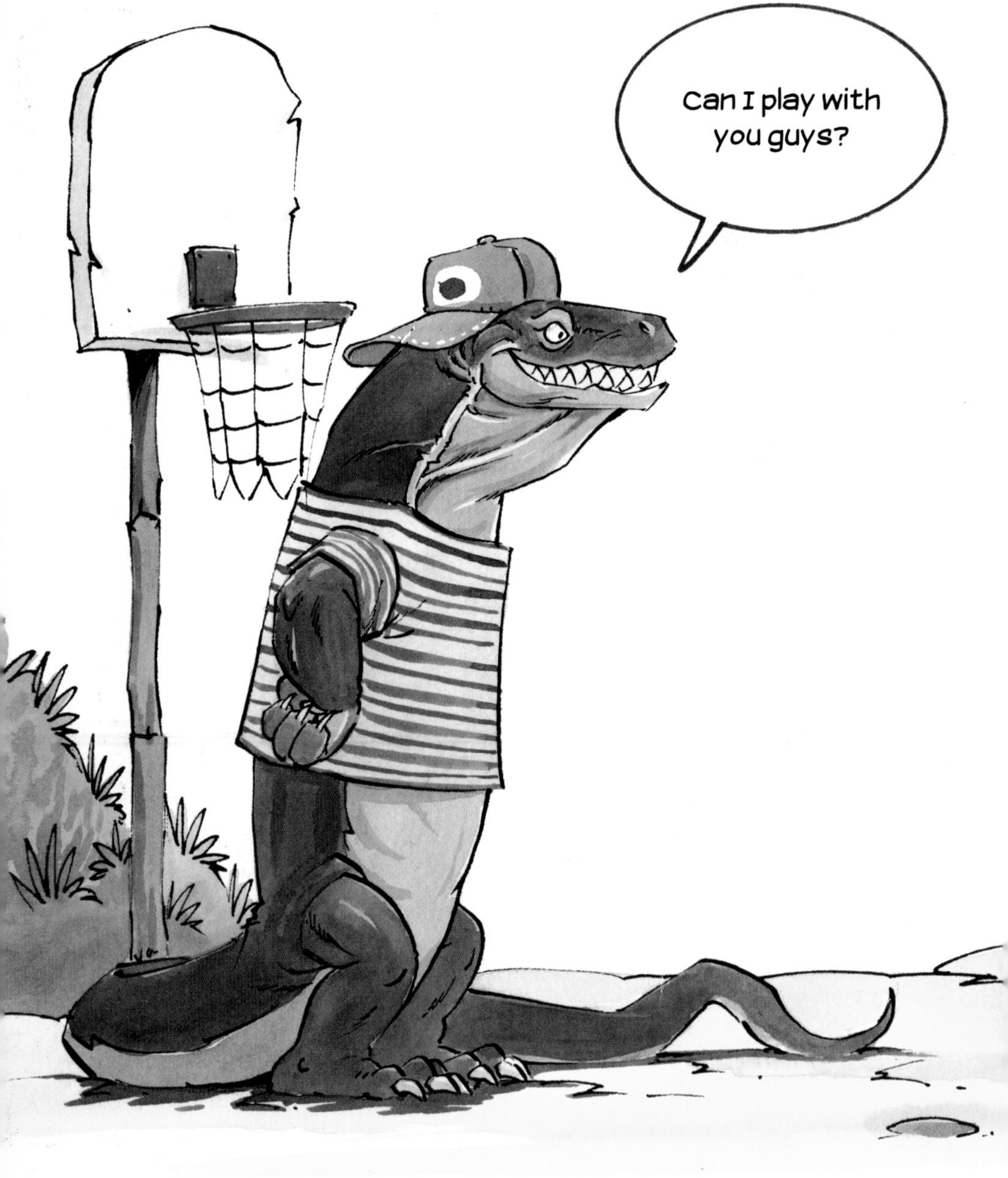
Can I play with you guys?

Komodo dragons are the largest lizards in the world. Some can measure over 3 metres (10 feet) in height and weigh 160 kilograms (350 pounds).

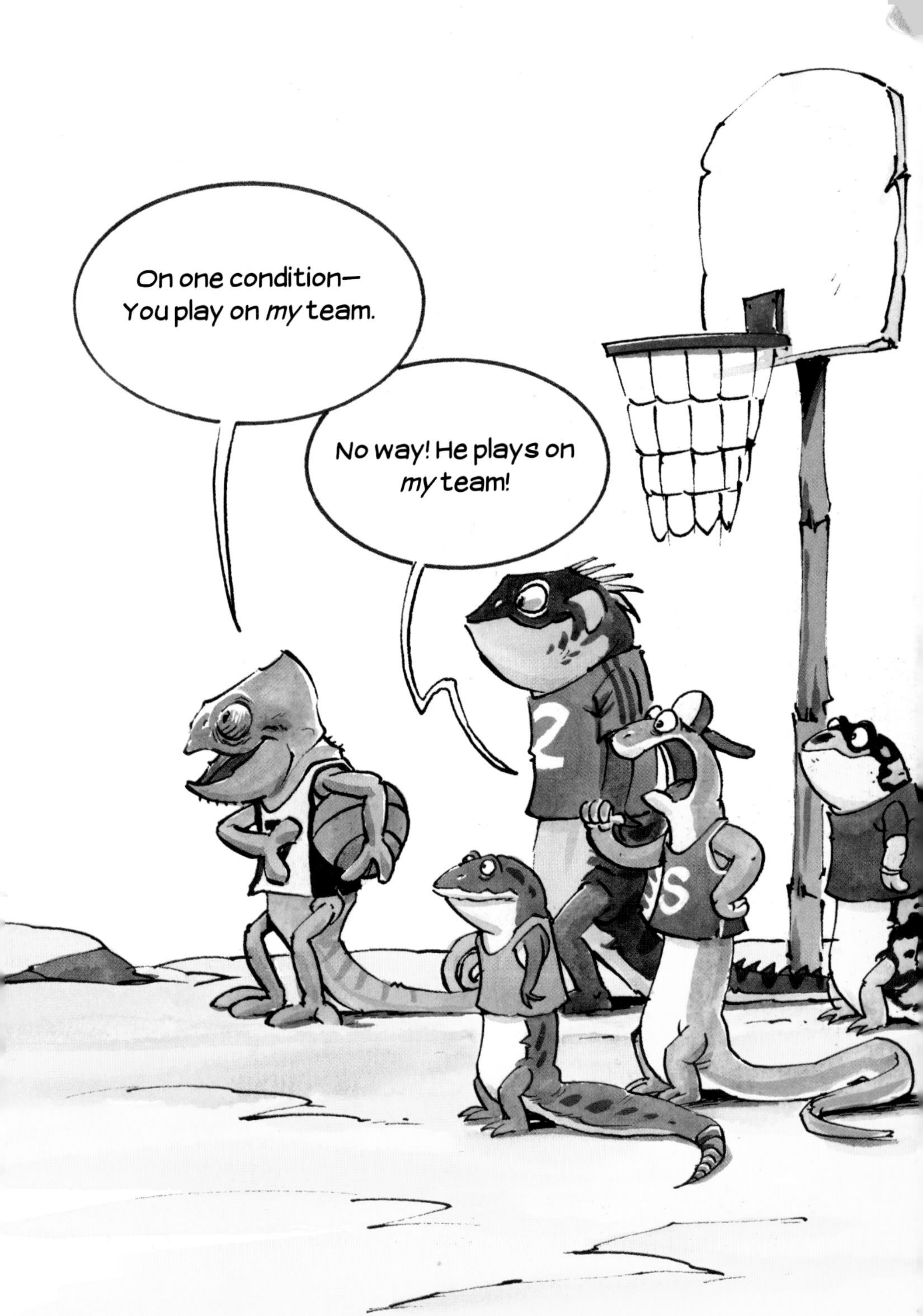
On one condition—
You play on *my* team.
No way! He plays on *my* team!

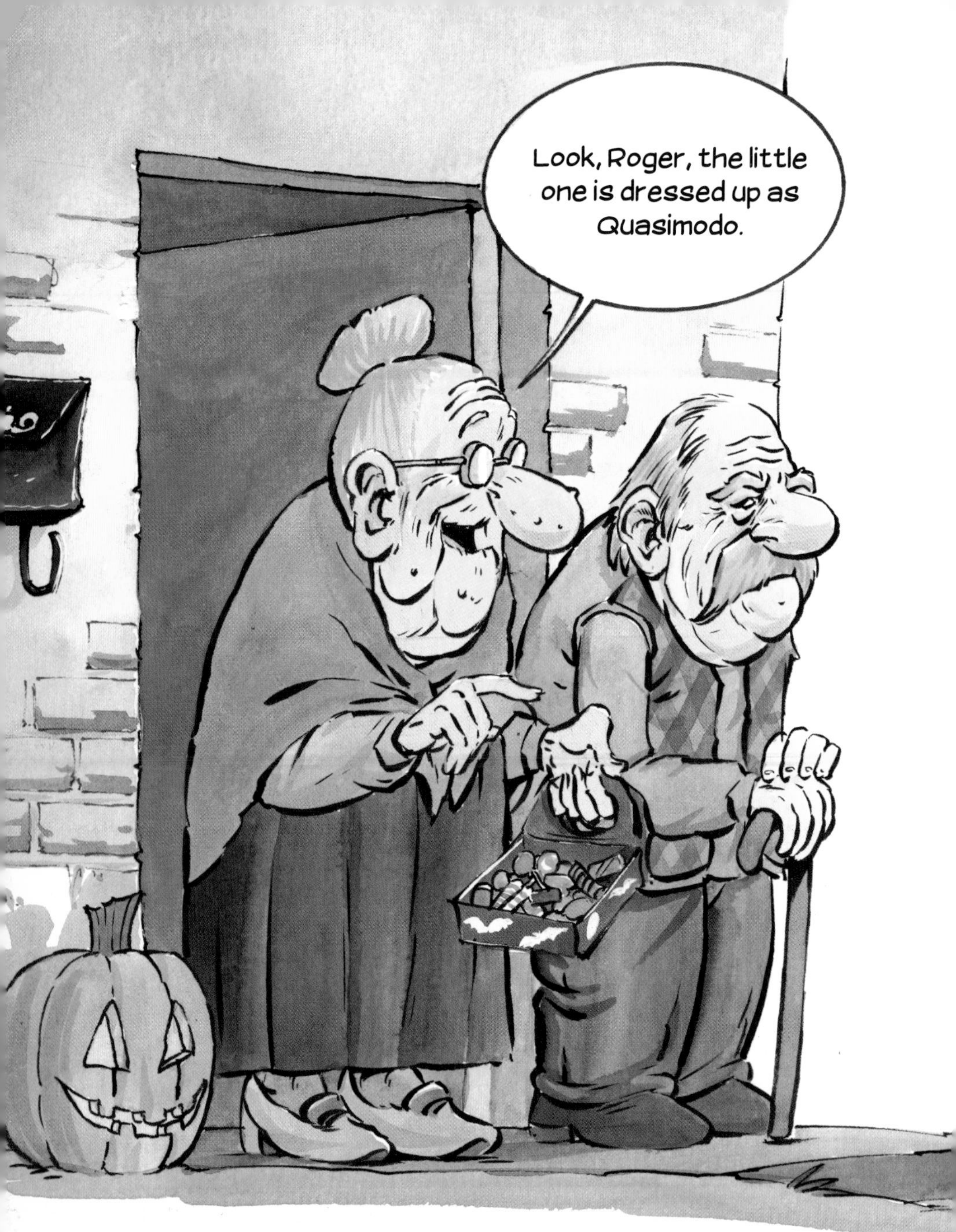
Look, Roger, the little one is dressed up as Quasimodo.

Komodo dragons are also known as Komodo monitors. They are found exclusively on small Indonesian islands, like Komodo Island.

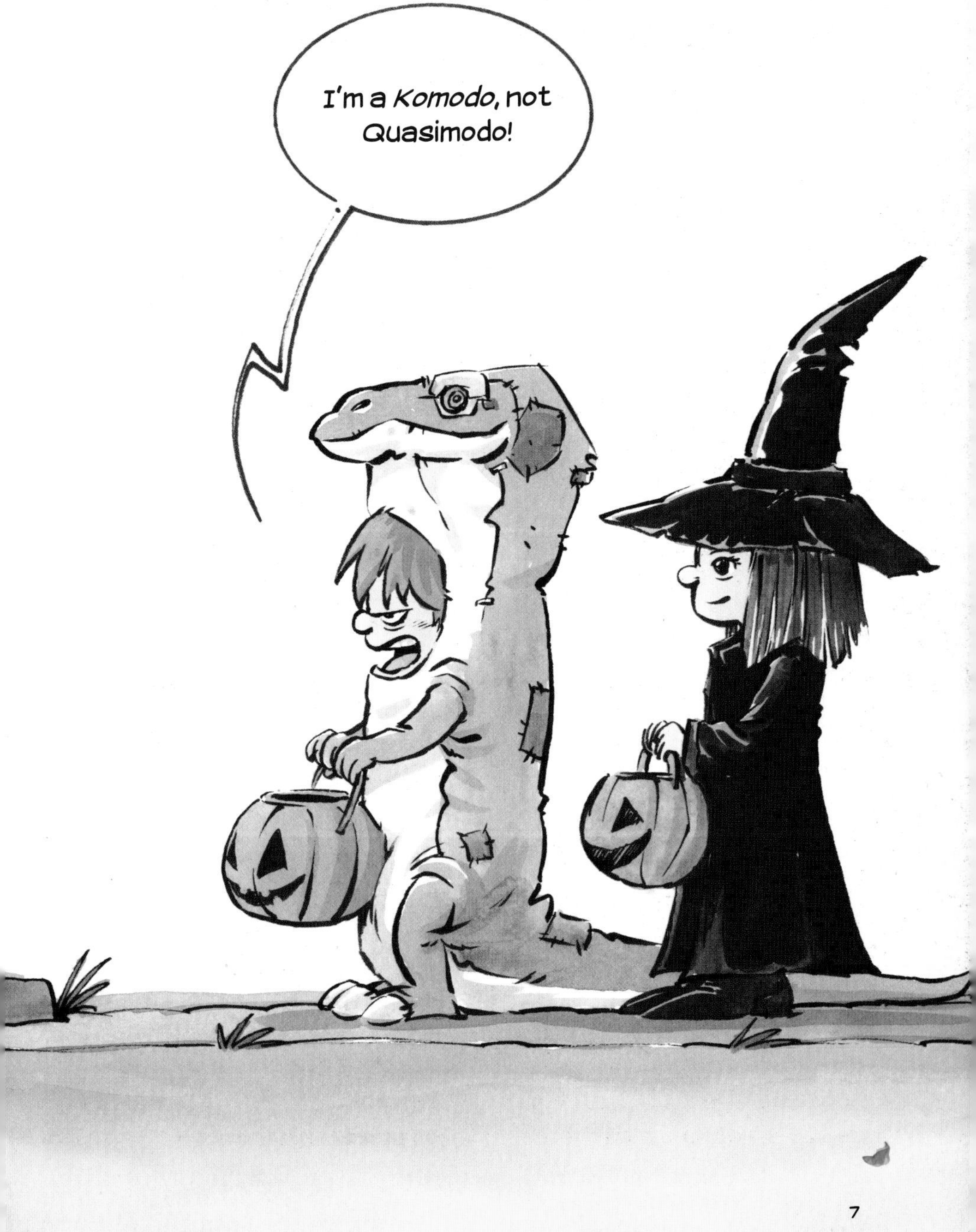
I'm a *Komodo*, not Quasimodo!

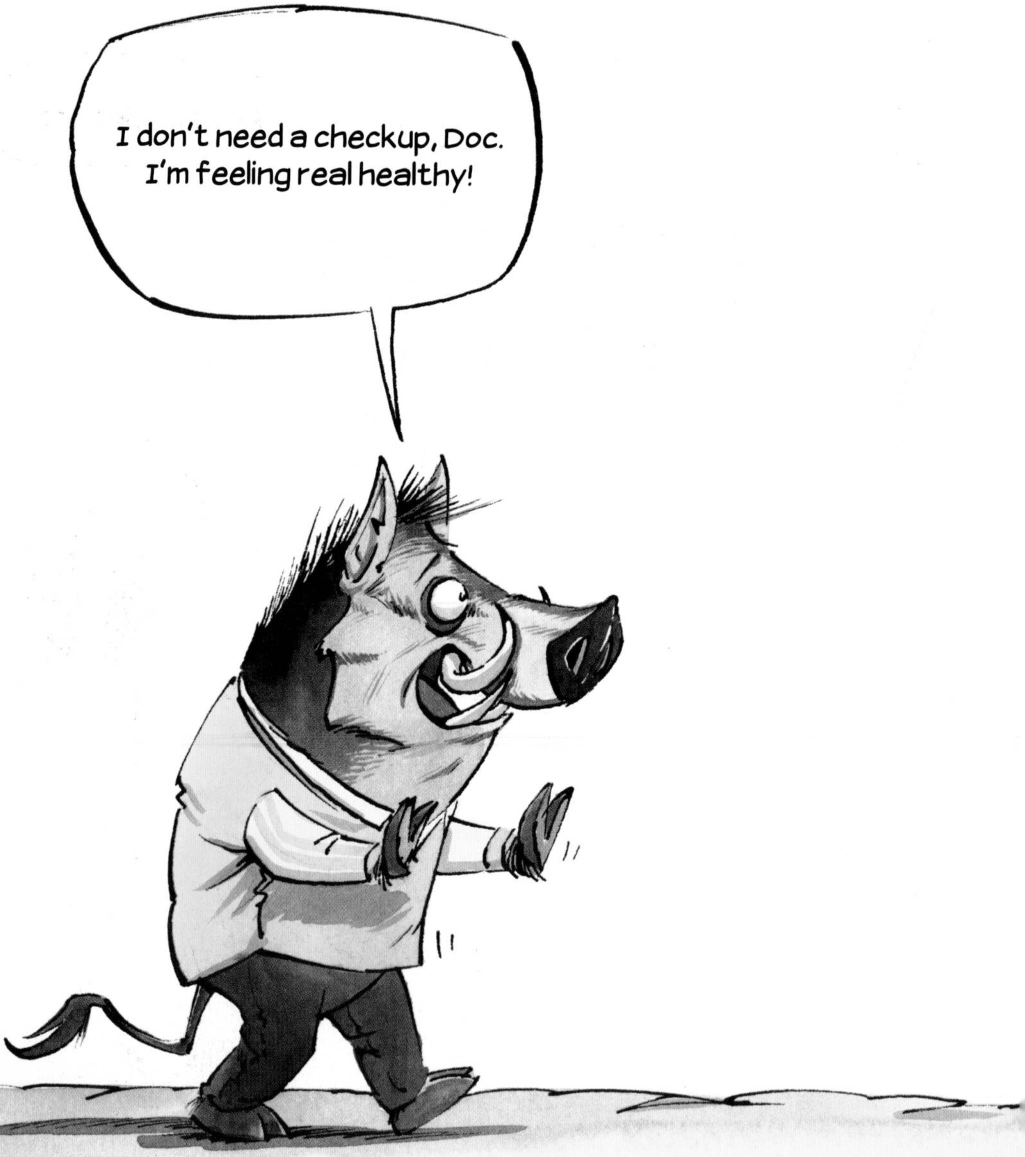
I don't need a checkup, Doc.
I'm feeling real healthy!

As both a **scavenger** and a super **predator**, this **carnivore** will eat dead animals and attack healthy live animals, too.

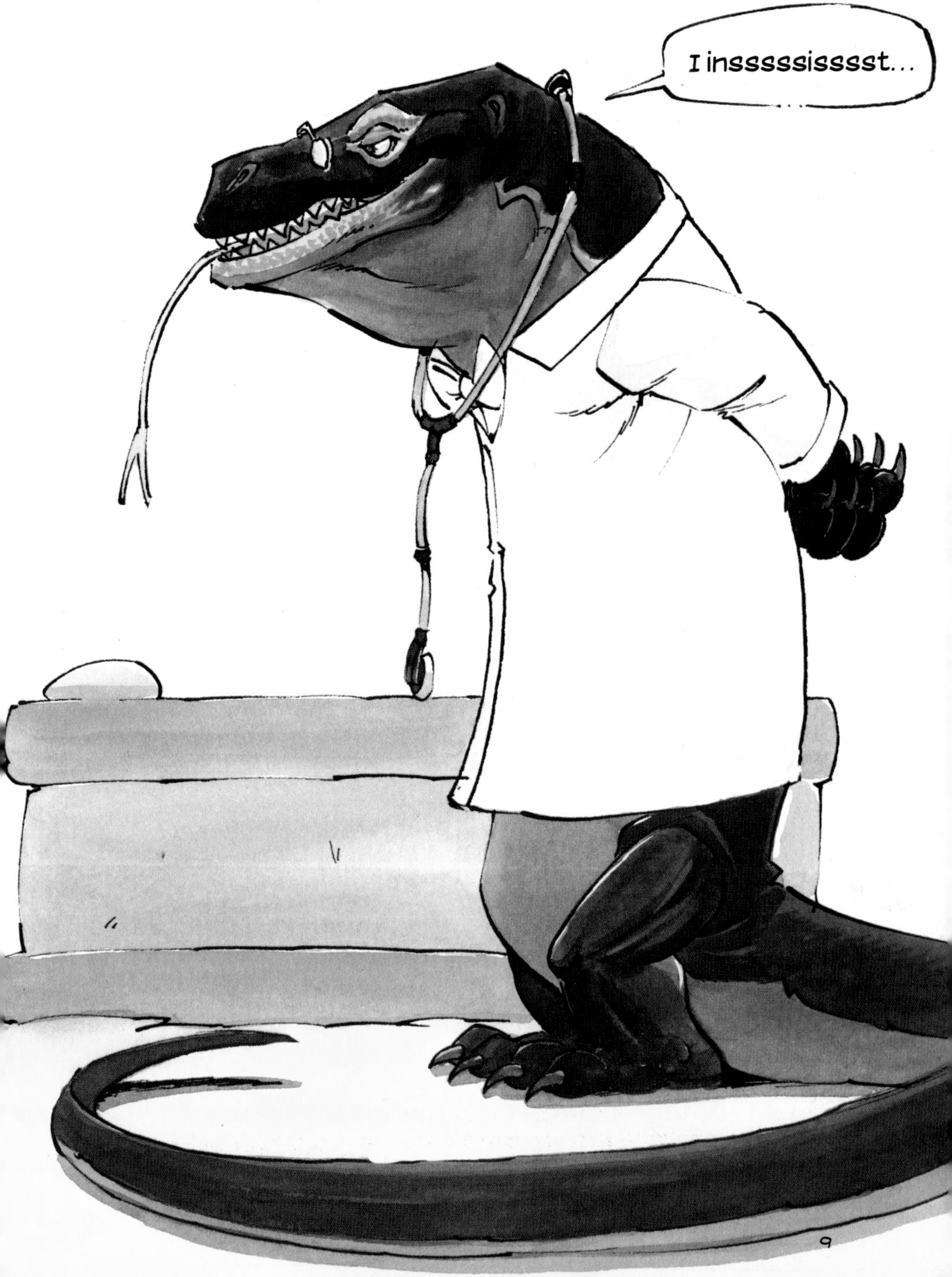
I insssssissssst...

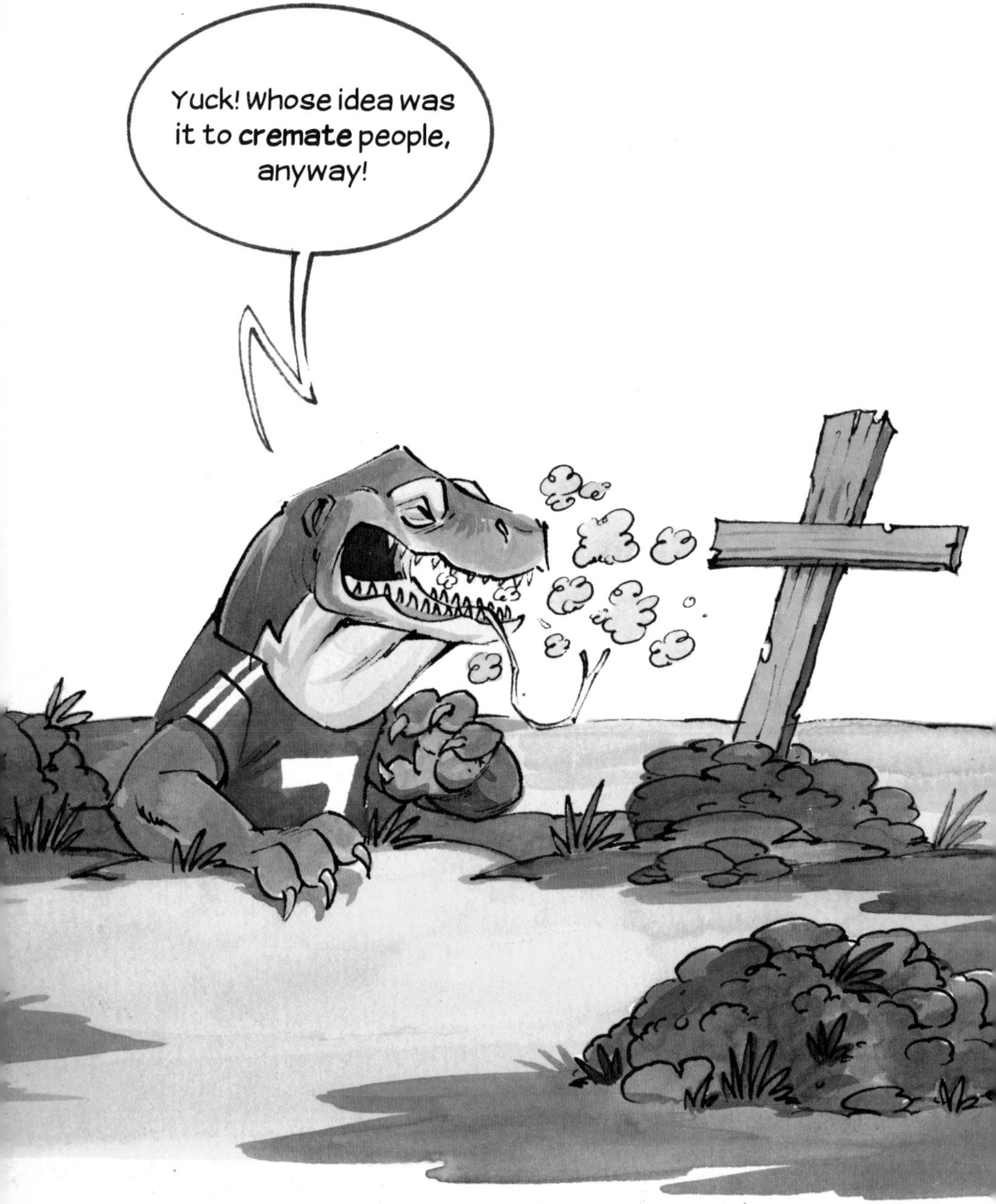
Yuck! Whose idea was it to **cremate** people, anyway!

The inhabitants of Komodo Island must bury their dead deep in the ground in order to prevent Komodo dragons from digging them up and eating them.

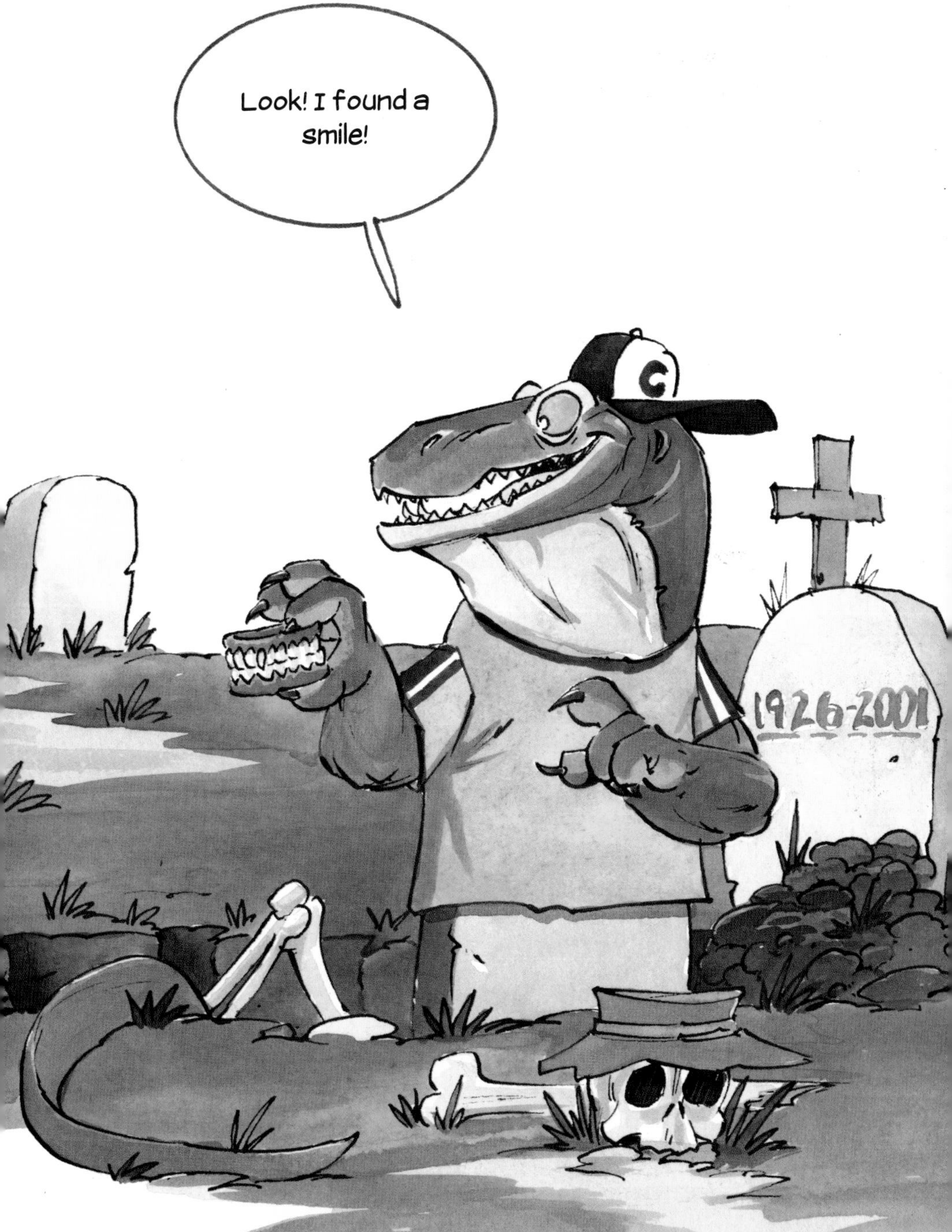
Look! I found a smile!
1926-2001

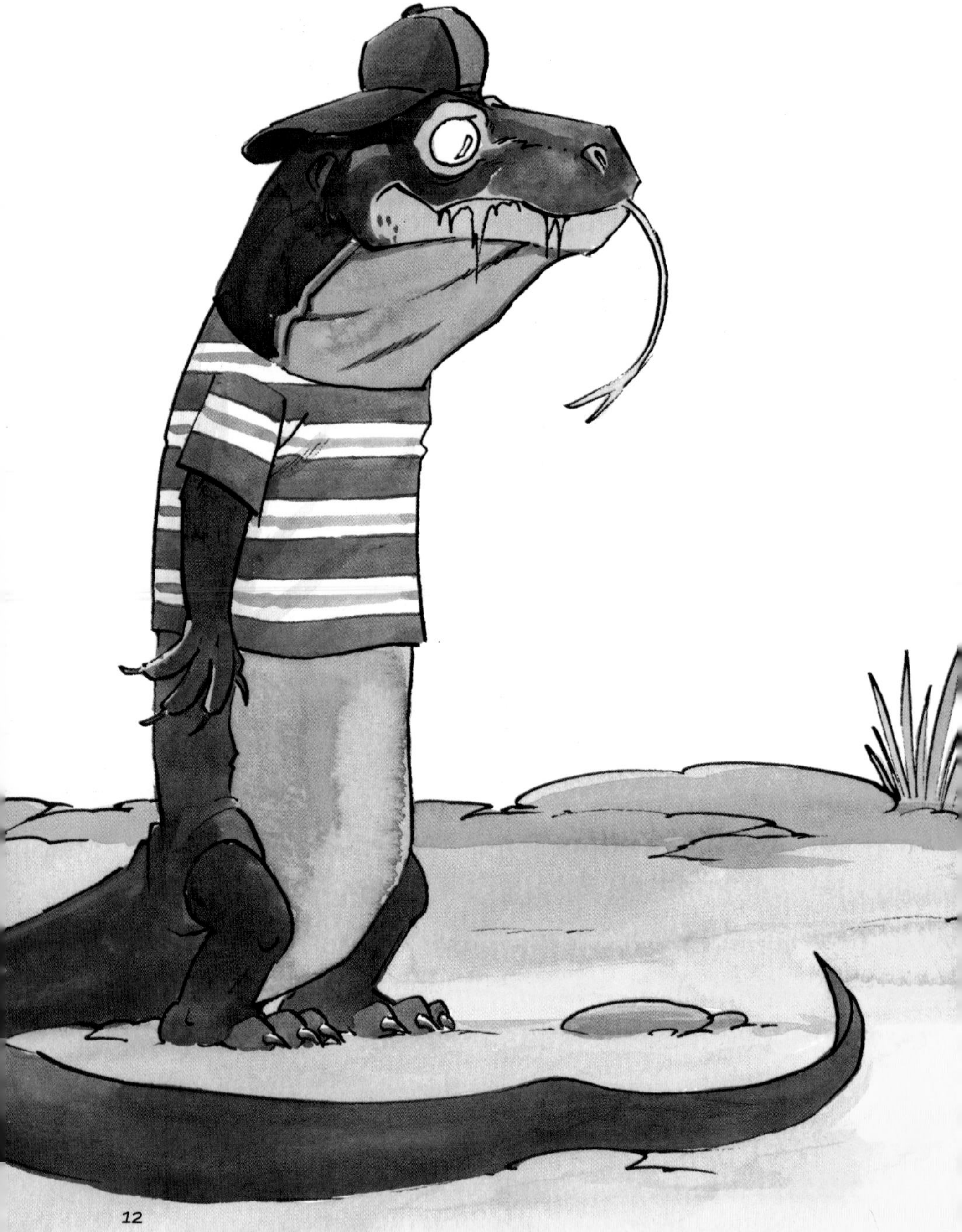

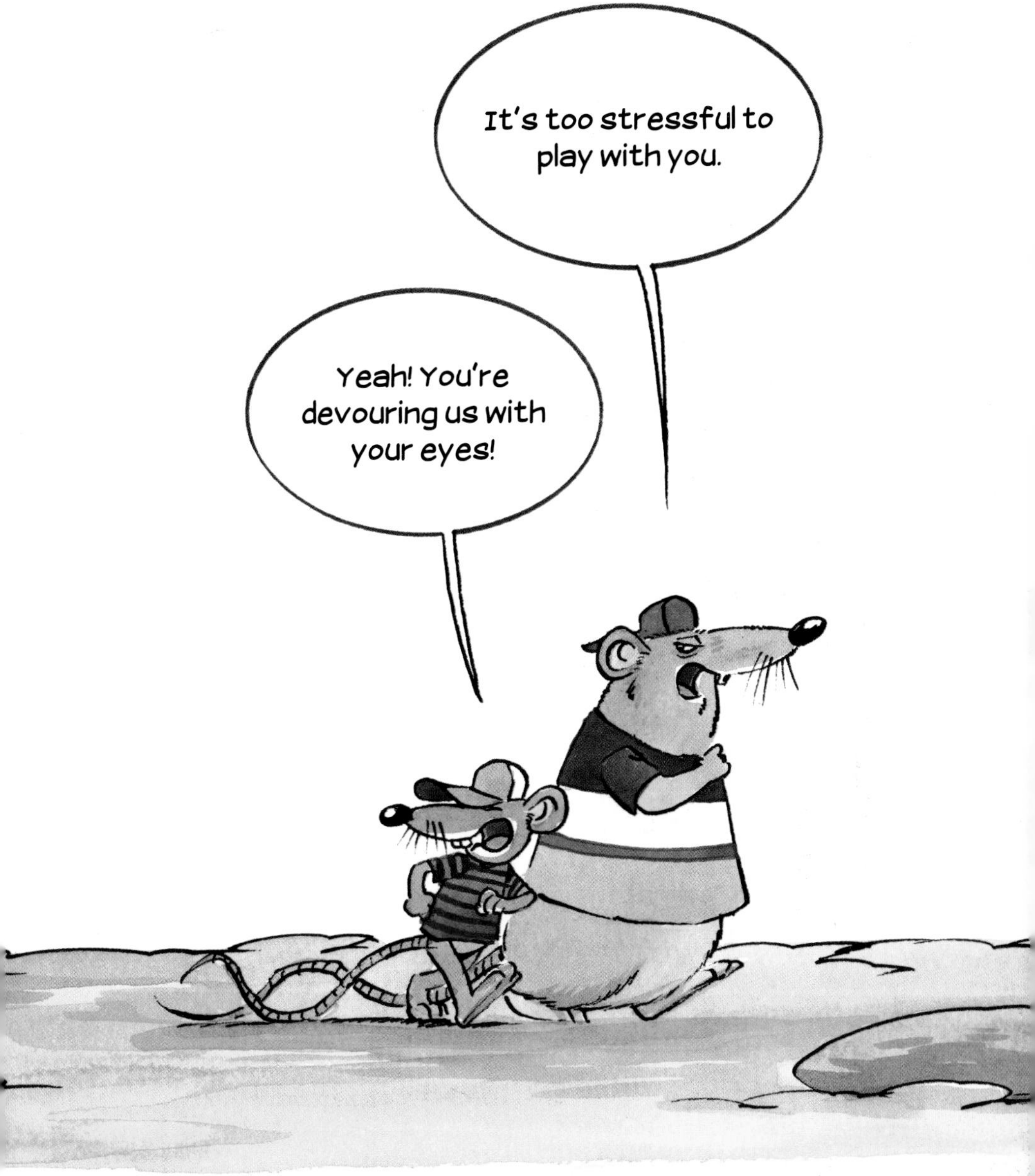
It's too stressful to play with you.
Yeah! You're devouring us with your eyes!

Young Komodo dragons eat small **mammals**, birds, **reptiles** and insects. Adults eat anything they can catch.

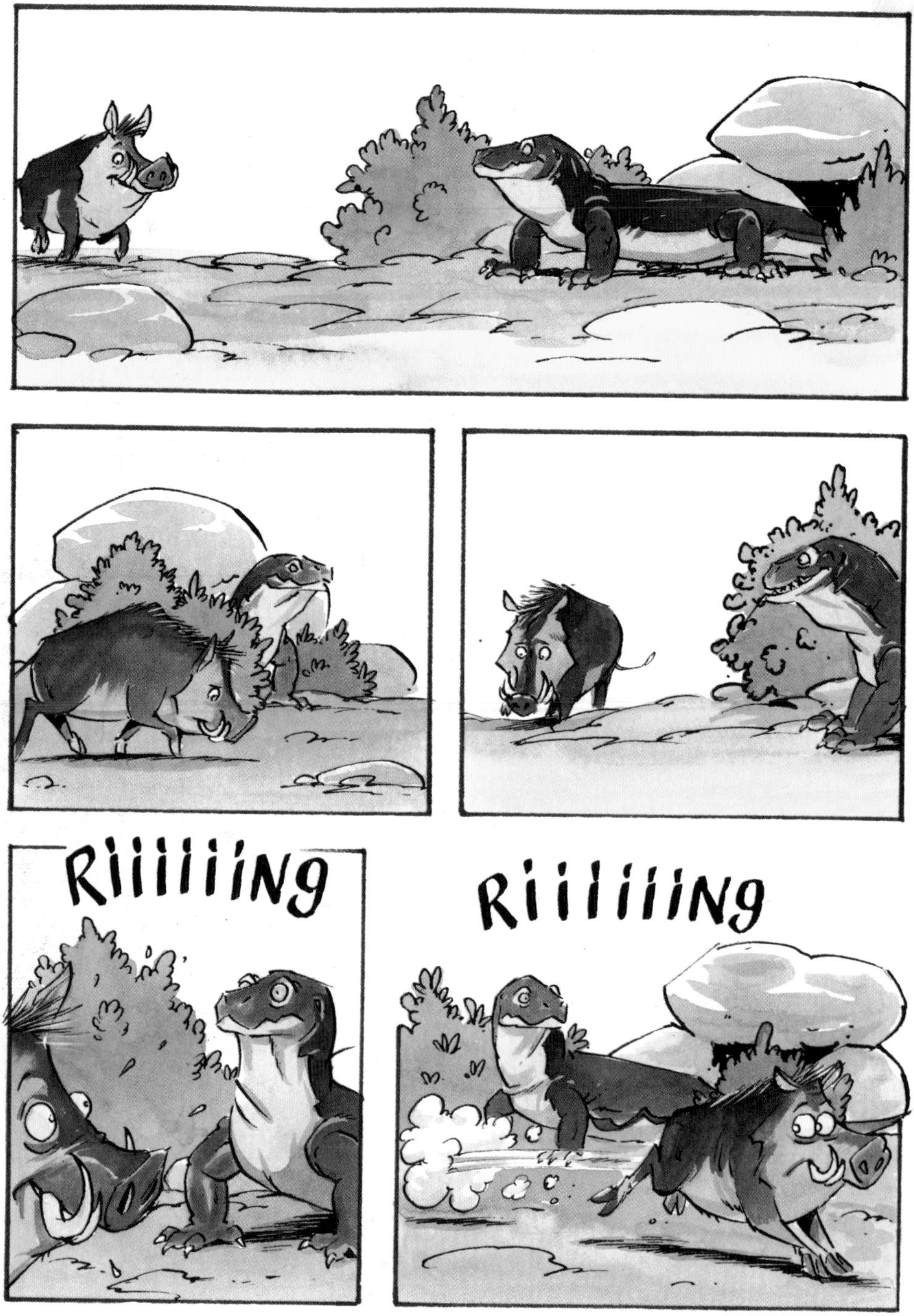
Riiiiiing
Riiiiiing

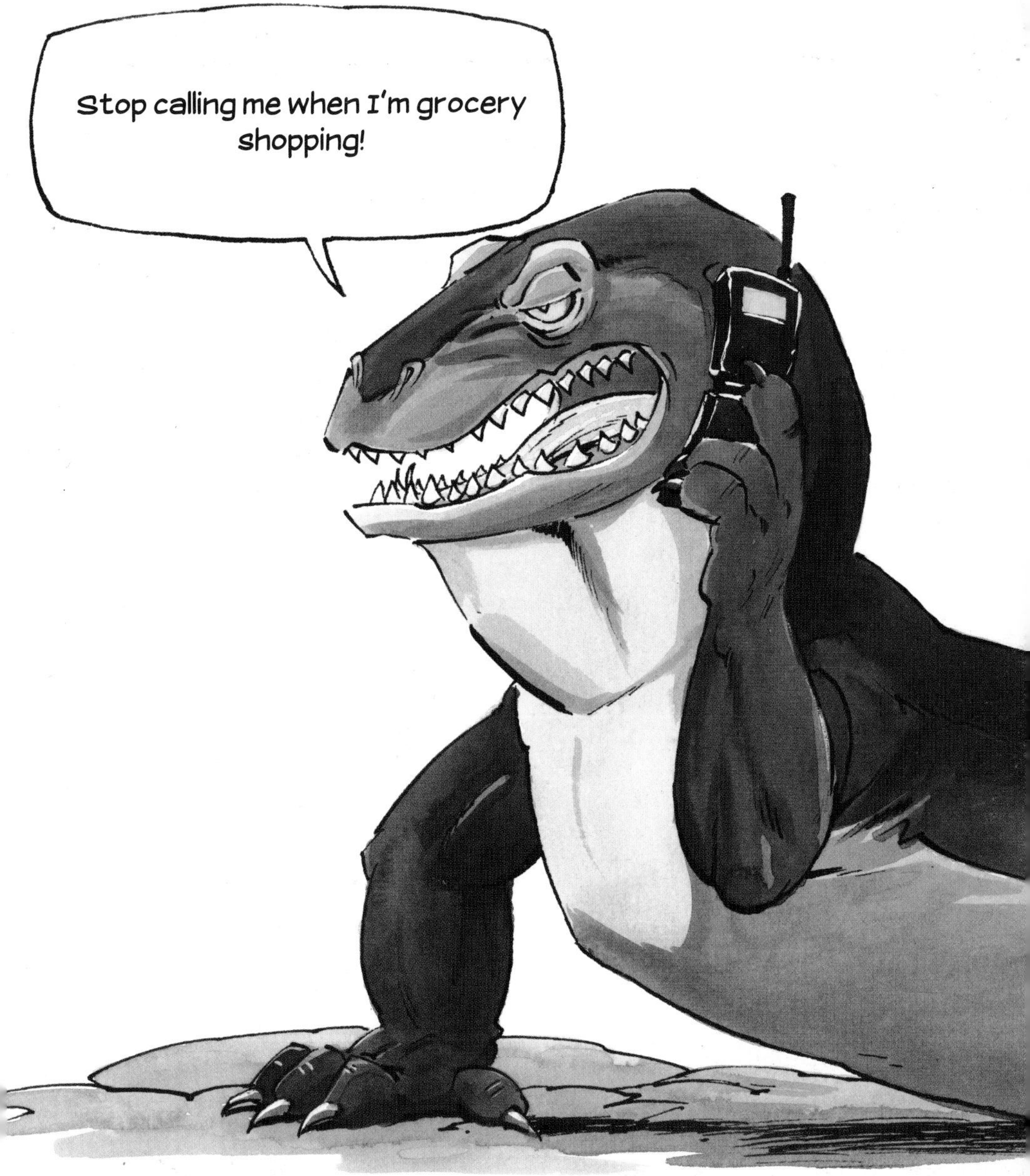
Stop calling me when I'm grocery shopping!

Komodo dragons often hunt by lying in wait. They can wait for hours before suddenly attacking **prey** that pass by.

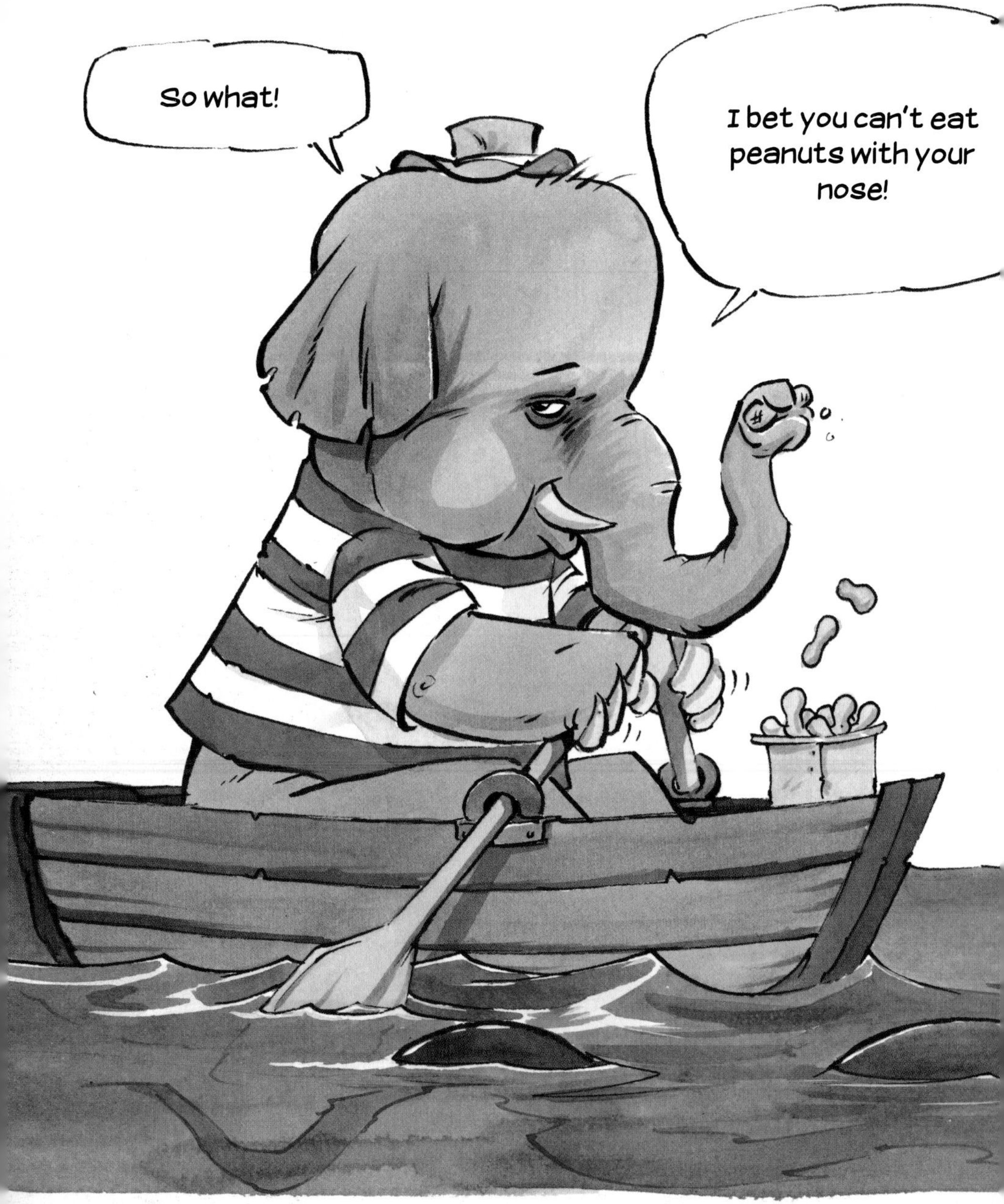
So what!
I bet you can't eat peanuts with your nose!

Despite their large size, these reptiles are fast and swift. They can run faster than 20 kilometres (12 miles) an hour for short distances. They are also excellent swimmers.

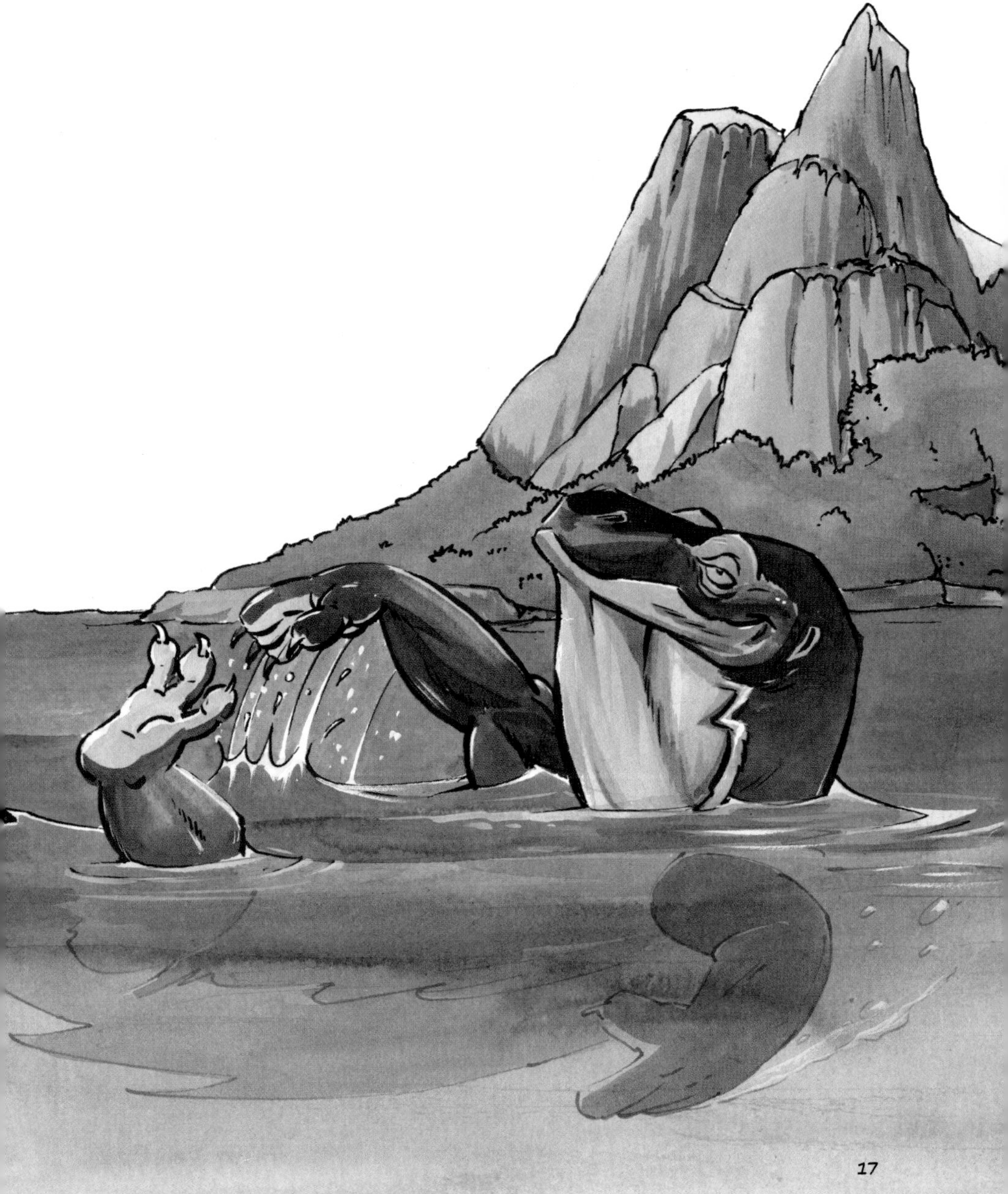

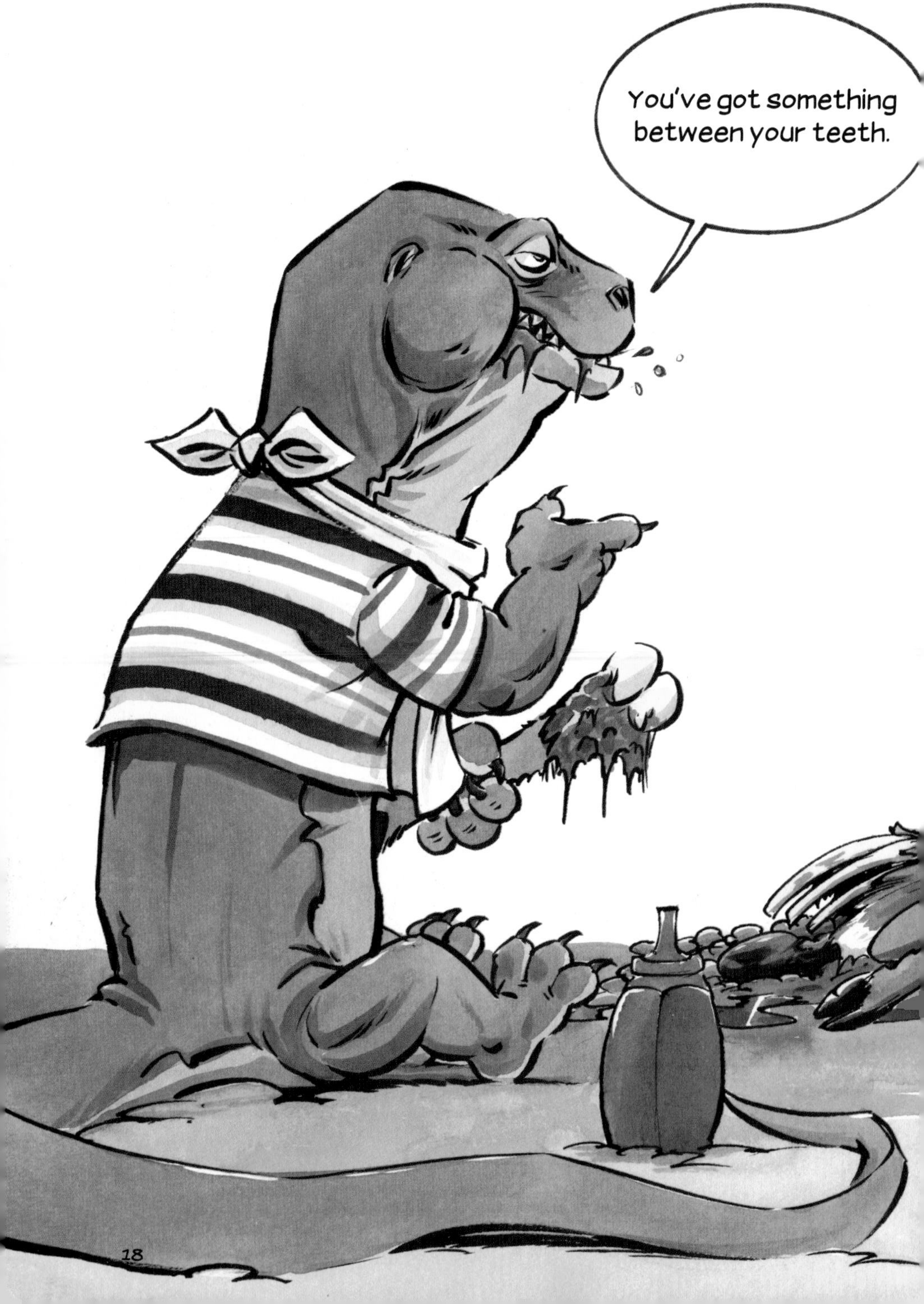
You've got something between your teeth.

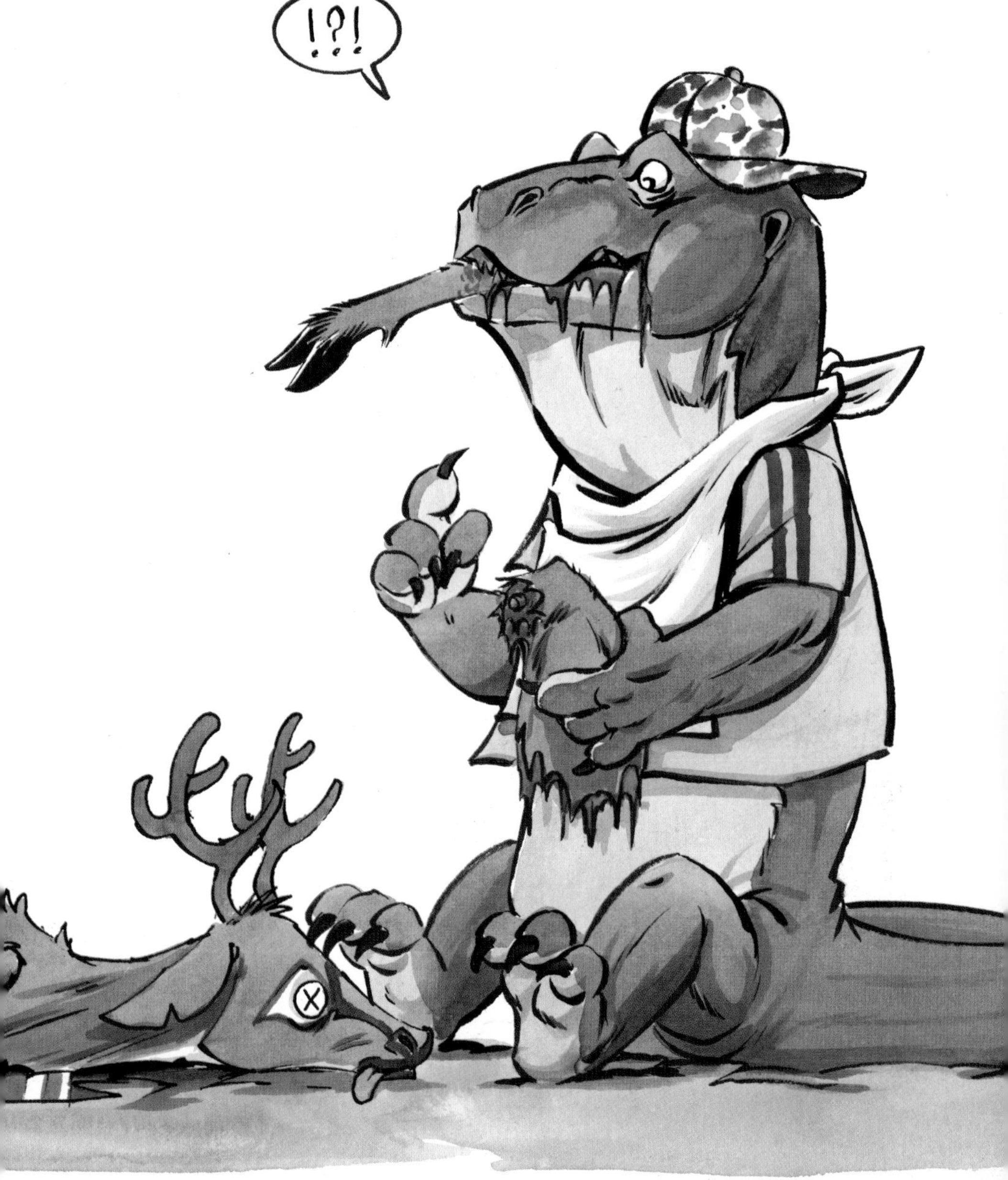
!?!

As an adult, the Komodo dragon is one of the most terrifying predators on the planet. It can crush a deer or a boar in just a few snaps of its powerful jaws.

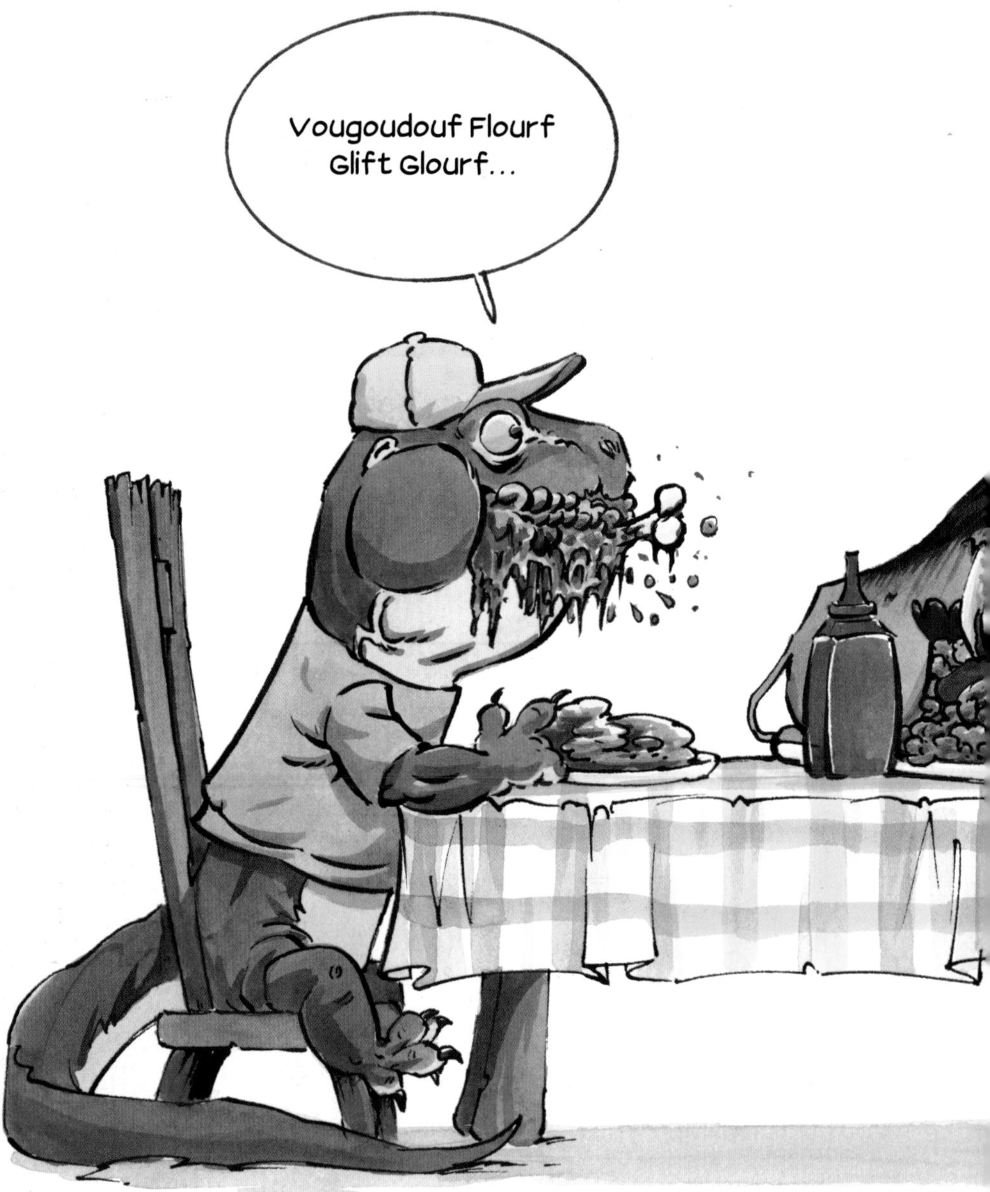
Vougoudouf Flourf
Glift Glourf...

The Komodo dragon's jagged teeth are curved backward, which helps the lizard hold onto its prey. Because its skull and jaw bones are so flexible, it can also chew its prey without opening its mouth widely, so the animal has no chance of escape.

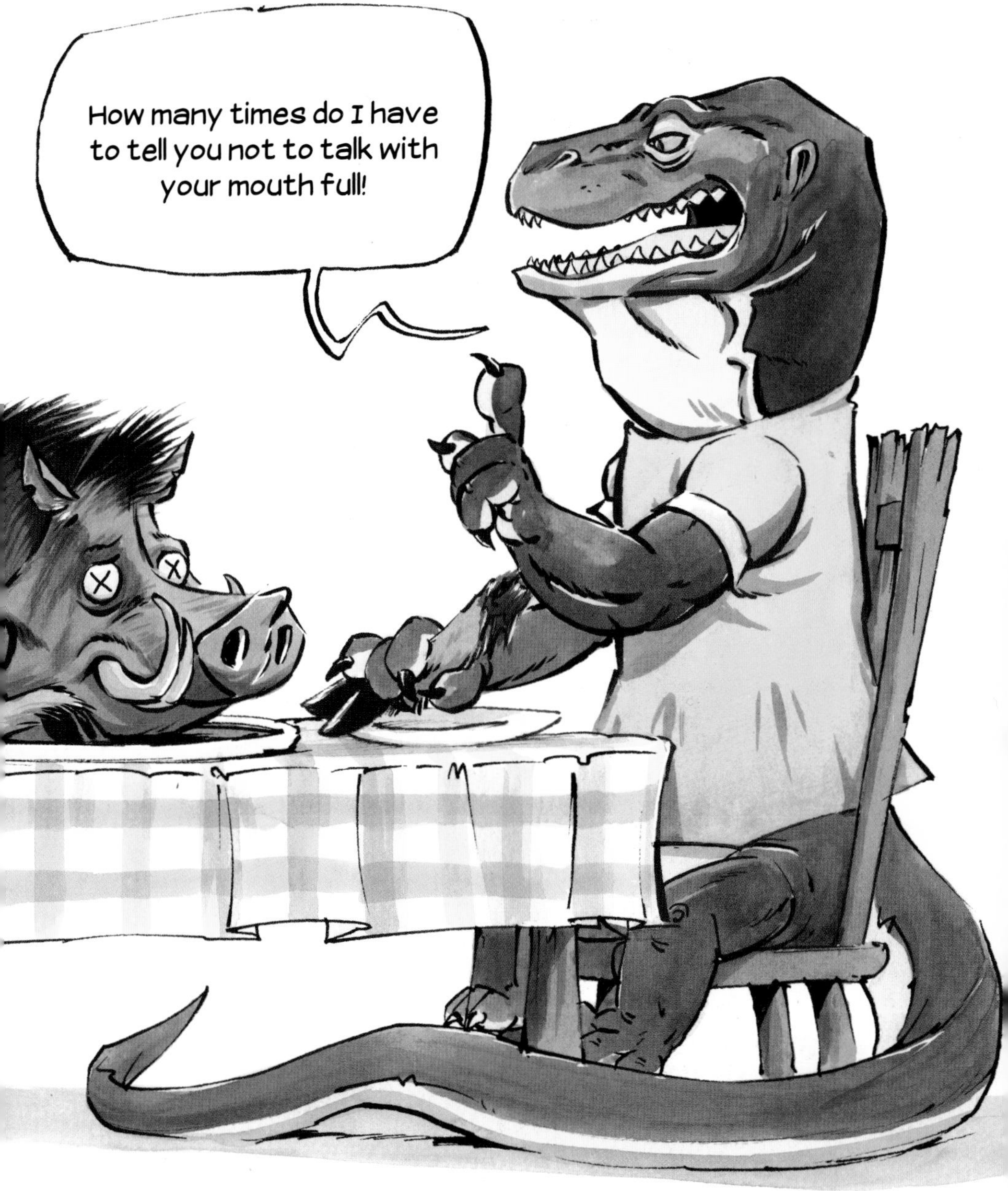
How many times do I have to tell you not to talk with your mouth full!

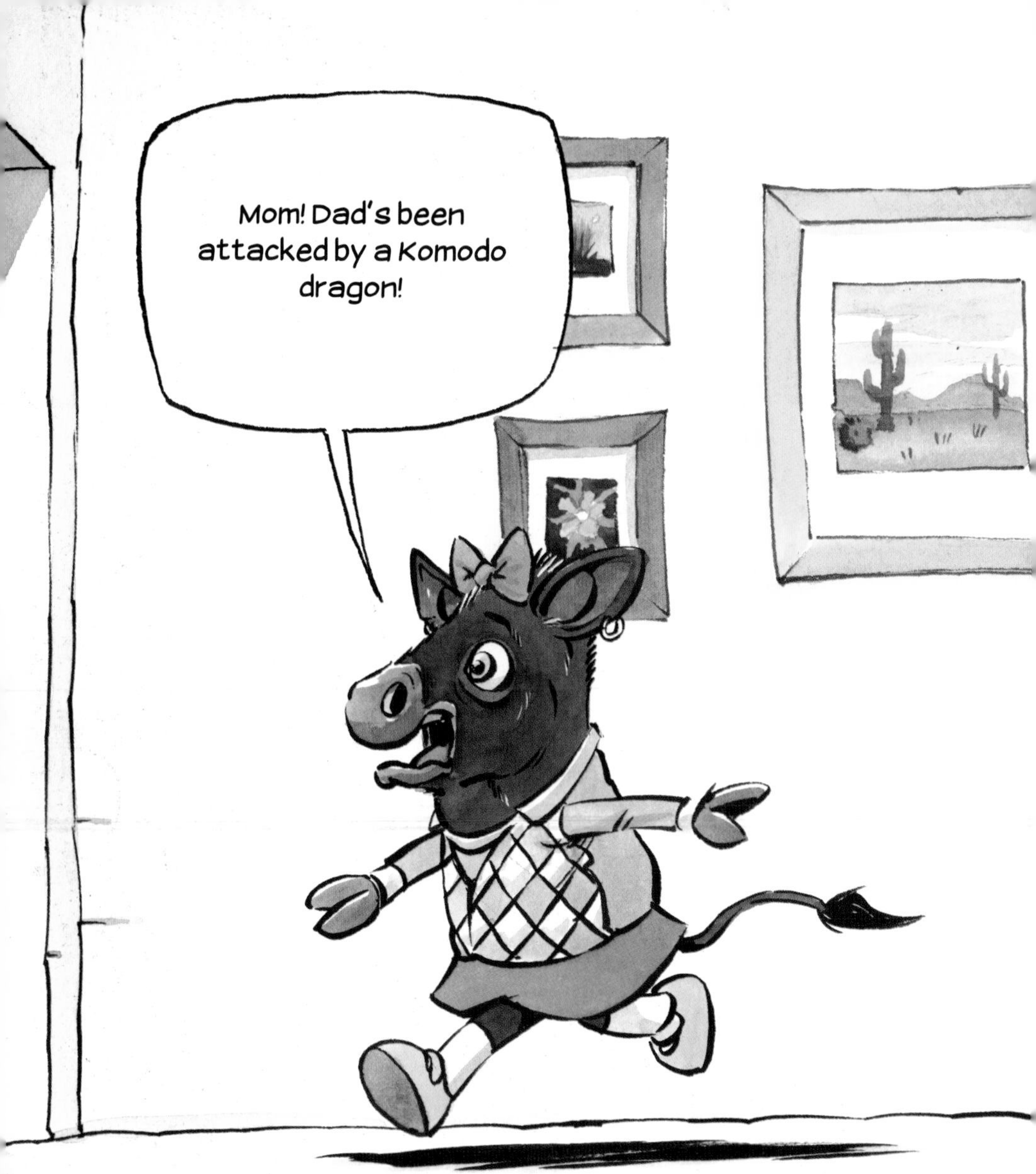
Mom! Dad's been attacked by a Komodo dragon!

Komodo dragons will shred apart large prey with their sharp teeth and long, powerful claws.

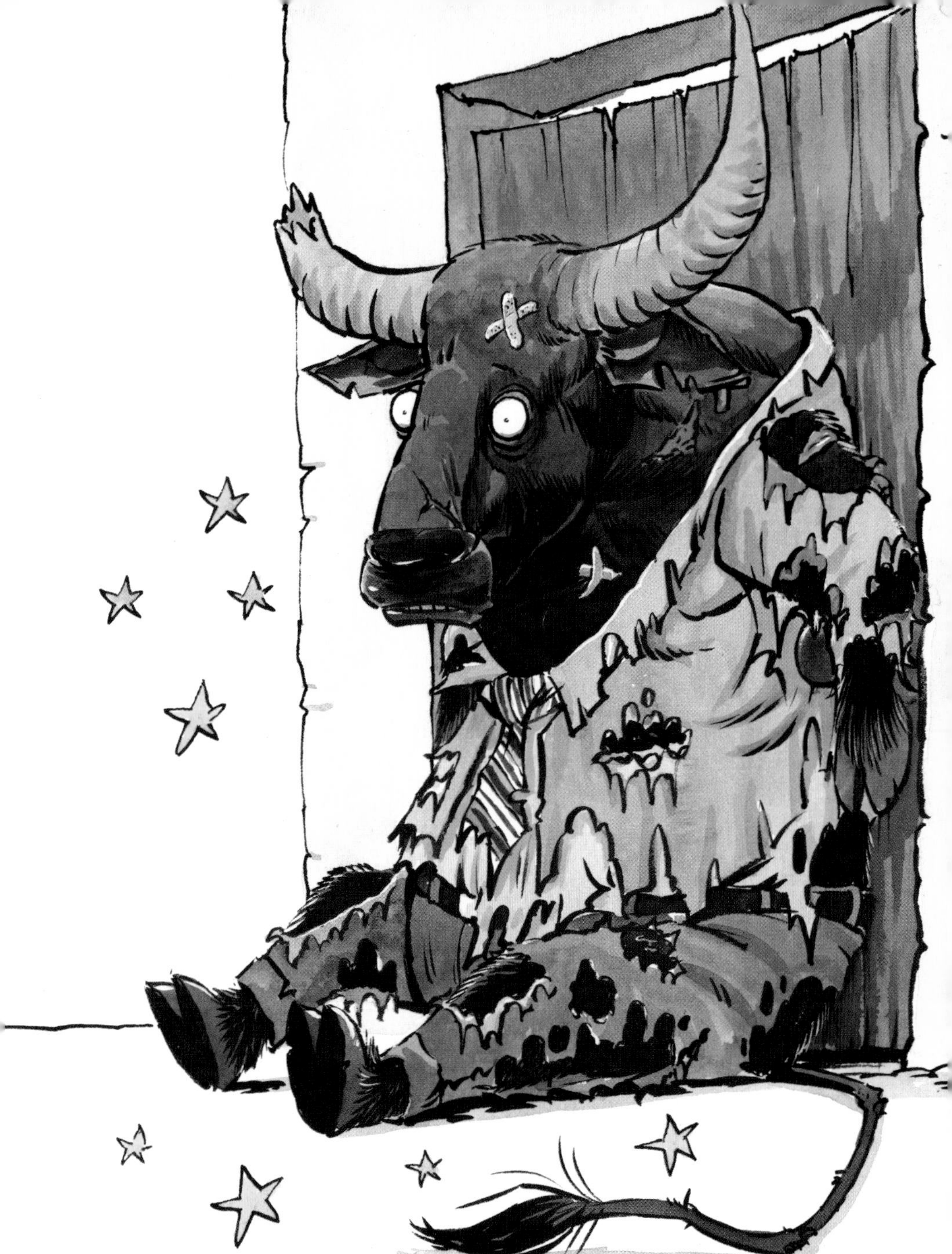

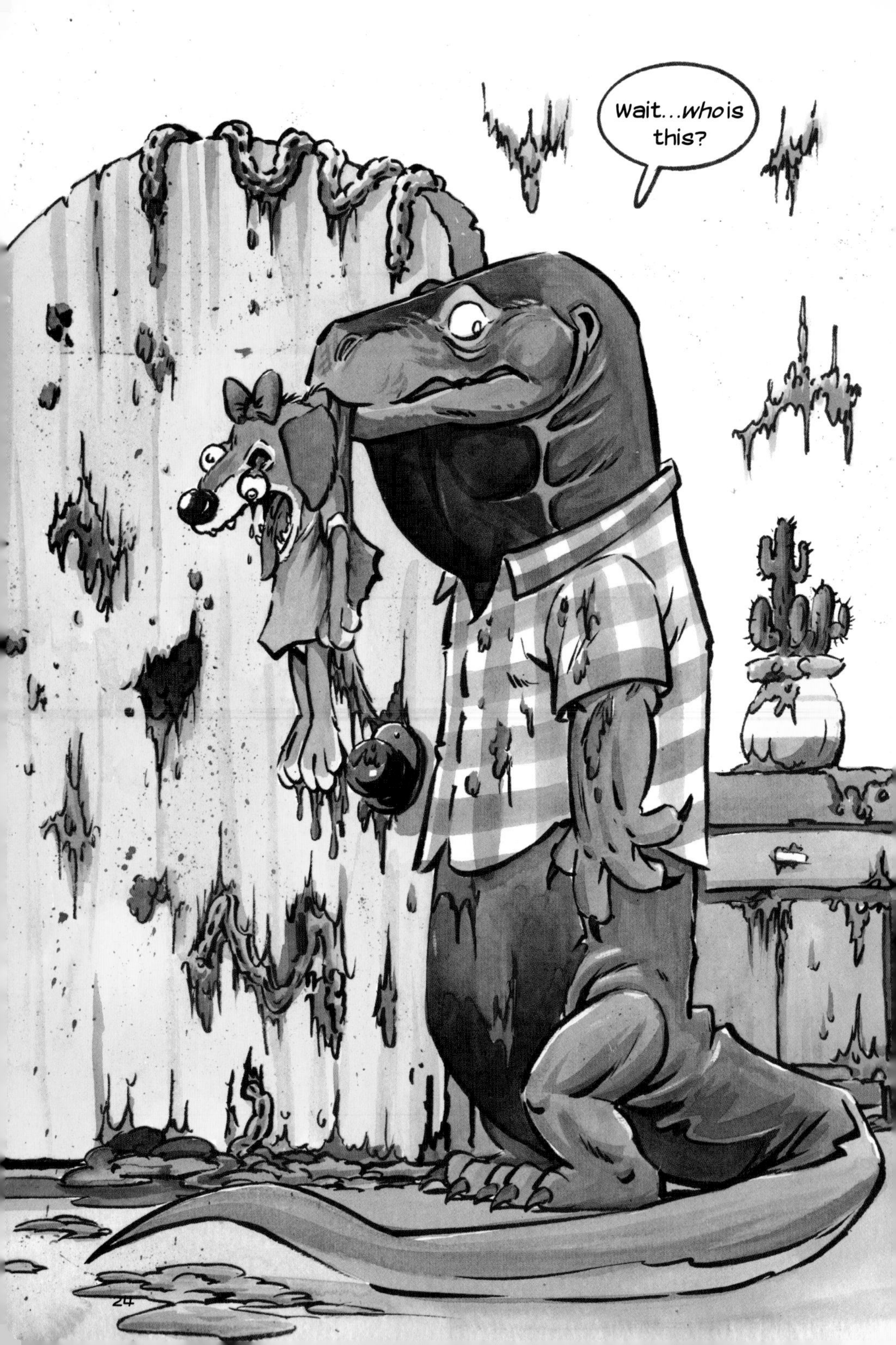
Wait...*who* is this?

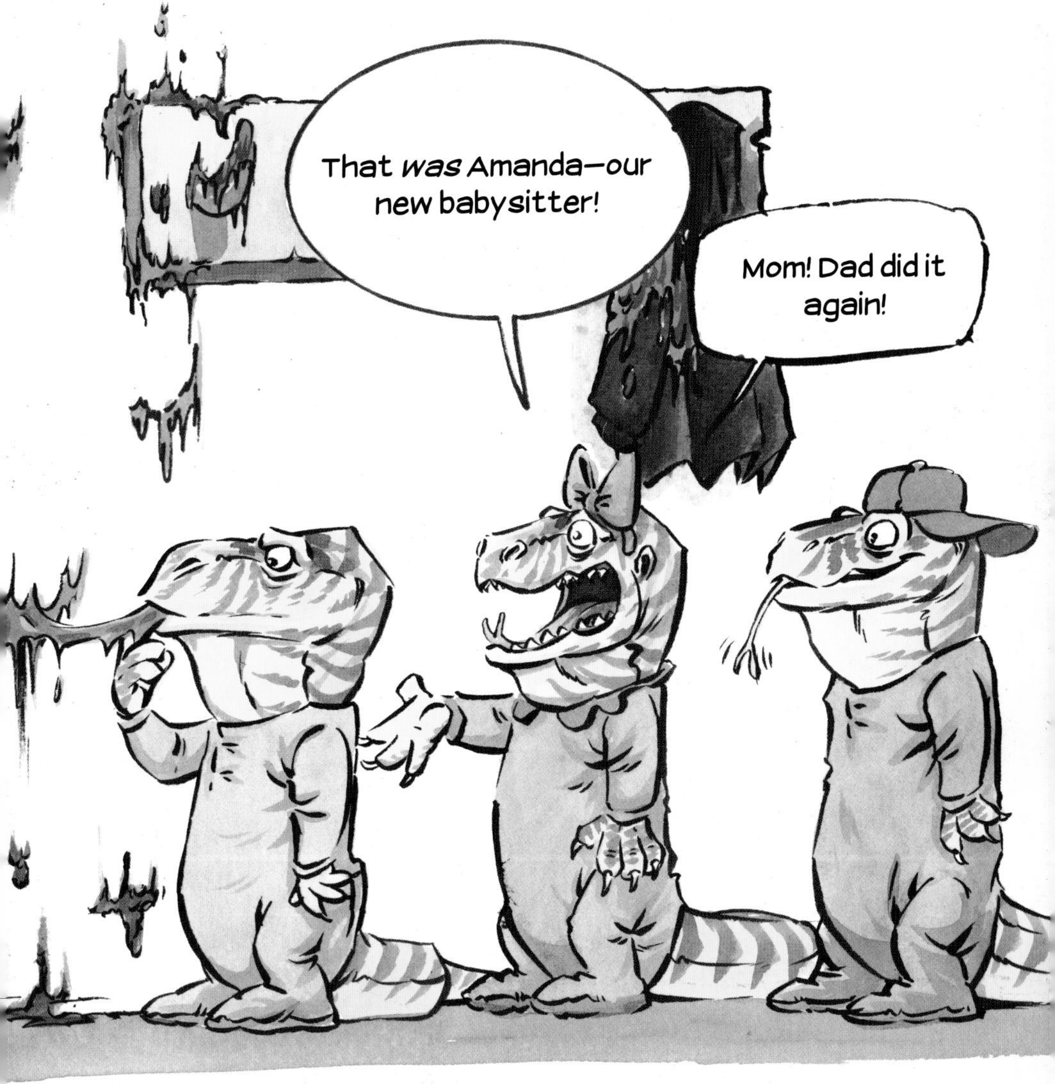
That *was* Amanda—our new babysitter!
Mom! Dad did it again!

Komodo dragons shake small prey with such energy that the animal's body will literally explode and release all of its organs.

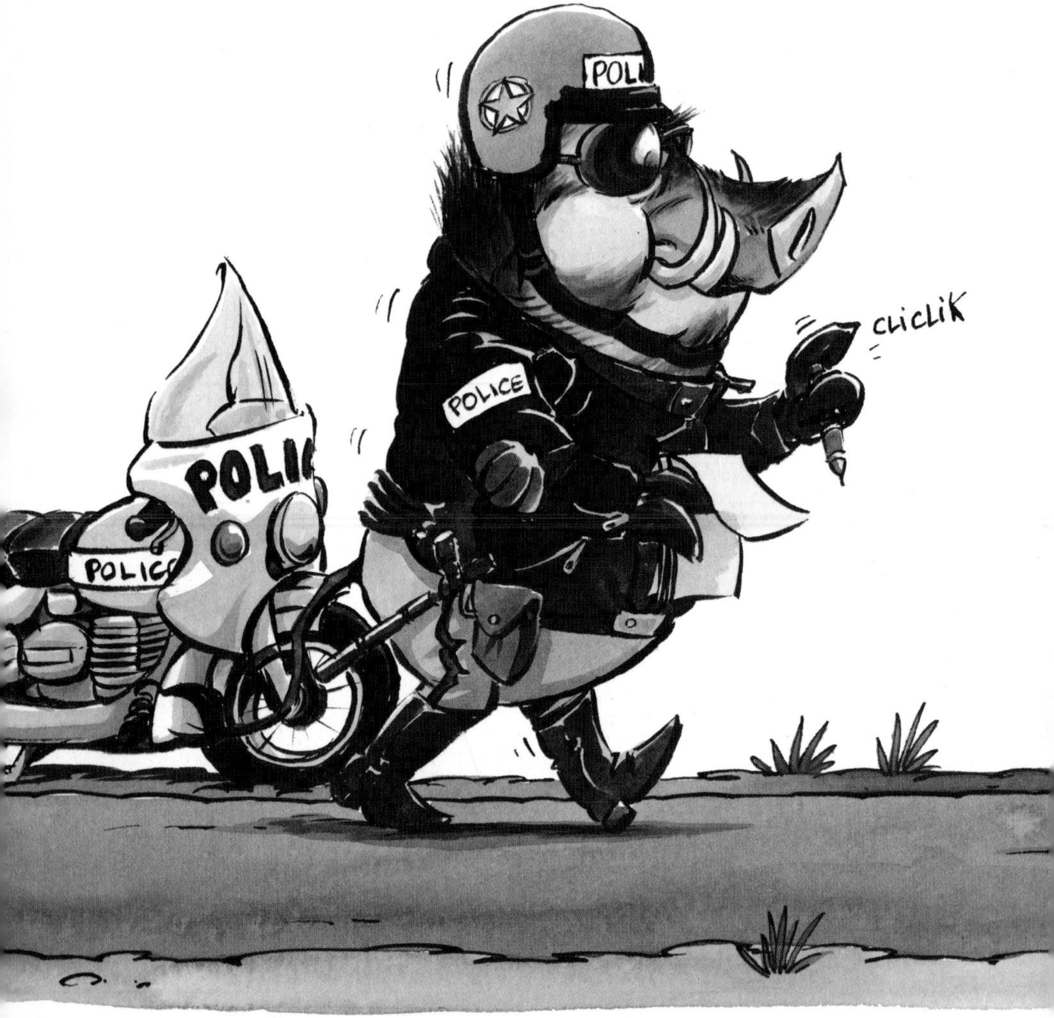
POL
POLICE
CLICLIK
POLIC
POLIC

In 15 minutes, a Komodo dragon can voraciously attack, kill, and devour a 30-kilogram (66-pound) boar.

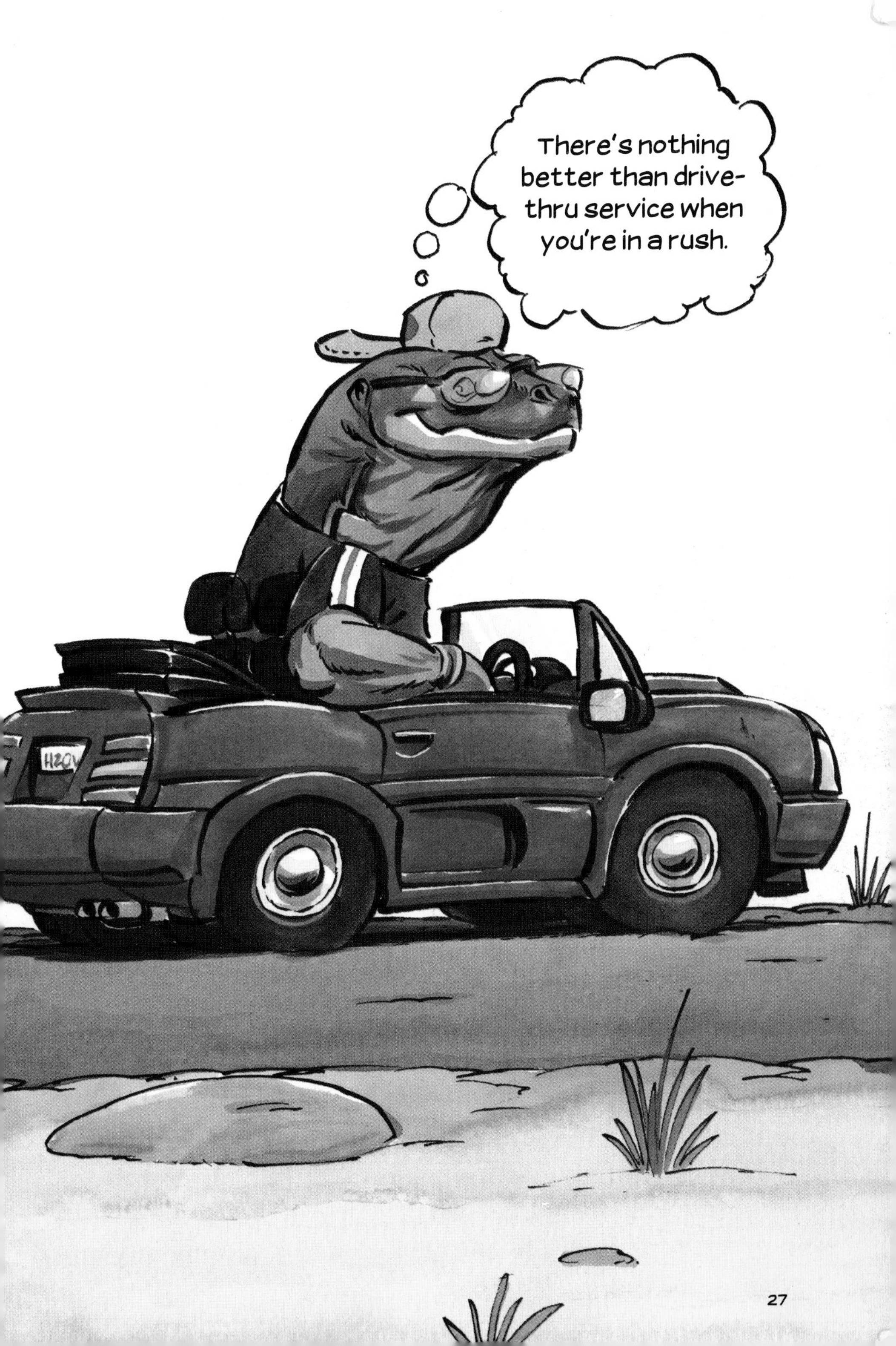
There's nothing better than drive-thru service when you're in a rush.
H2OV

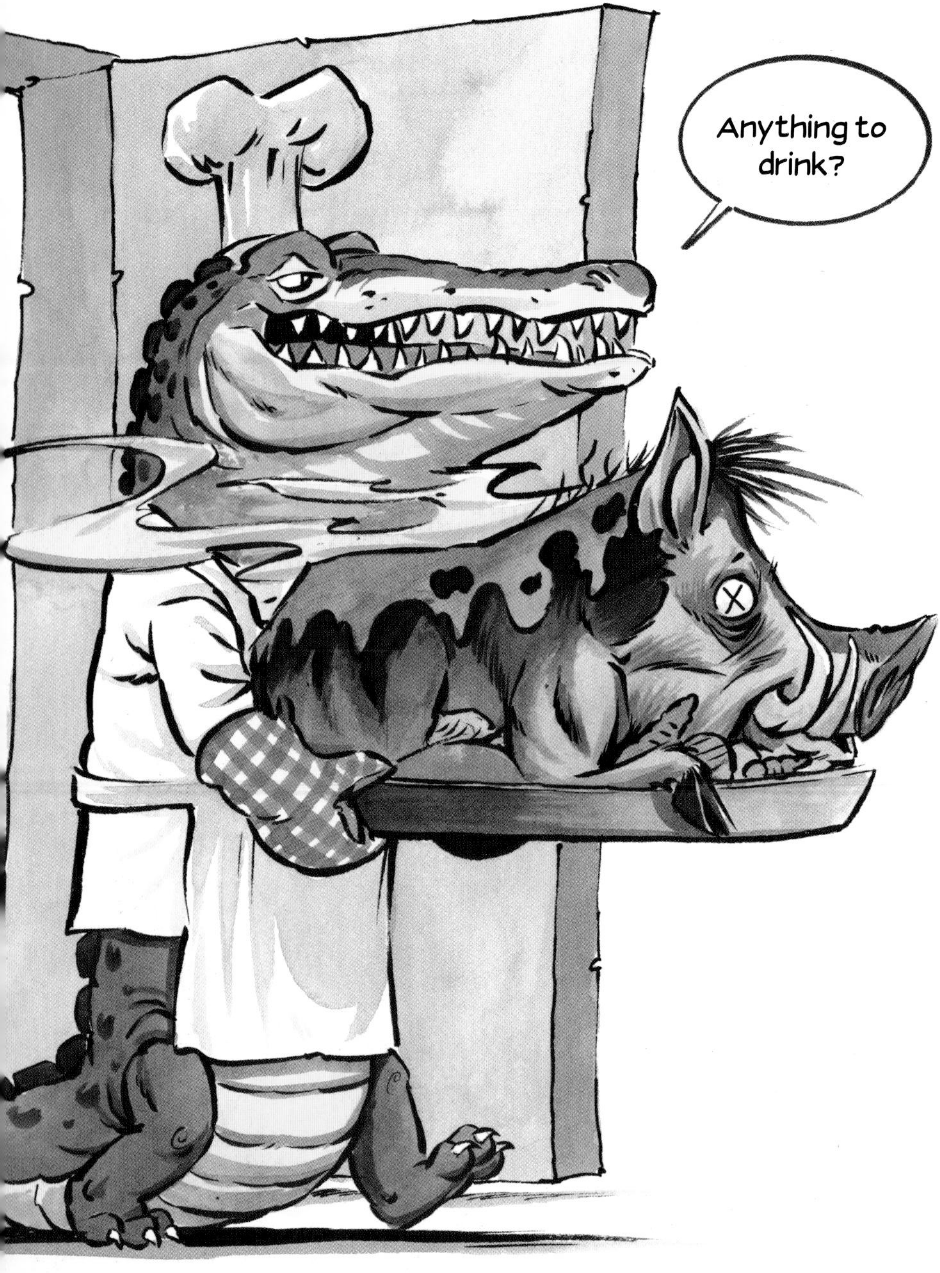
Anything to drink?

The Komodo dragon has such a large appetite that it can swallow up to 80% of its weight in a single meal. A 50-kilogram (110-pound) female was once seen eating a 44-kilogram (97-pound) boar.

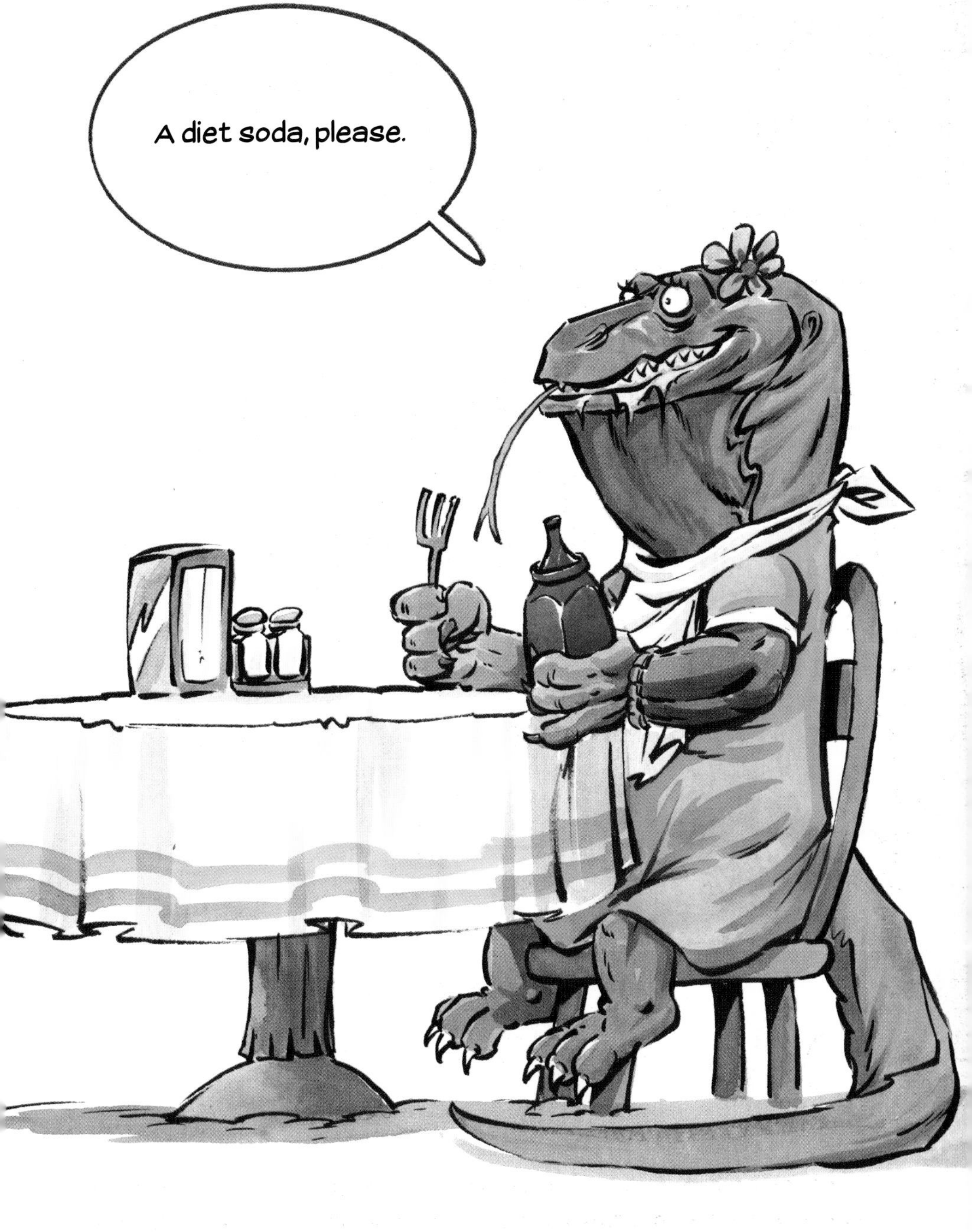
A diet soda, please.

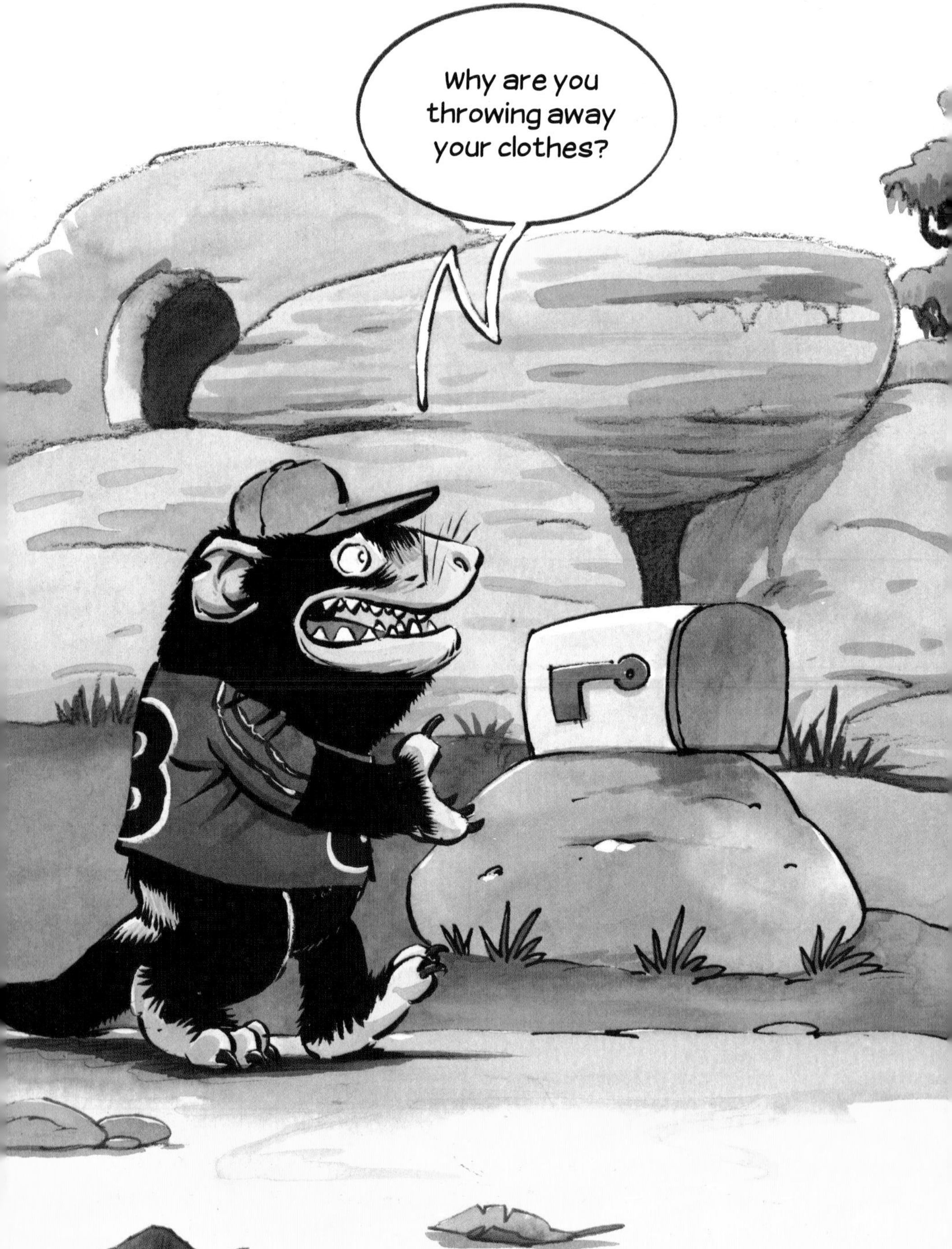
Why are you throwing away your clothes?

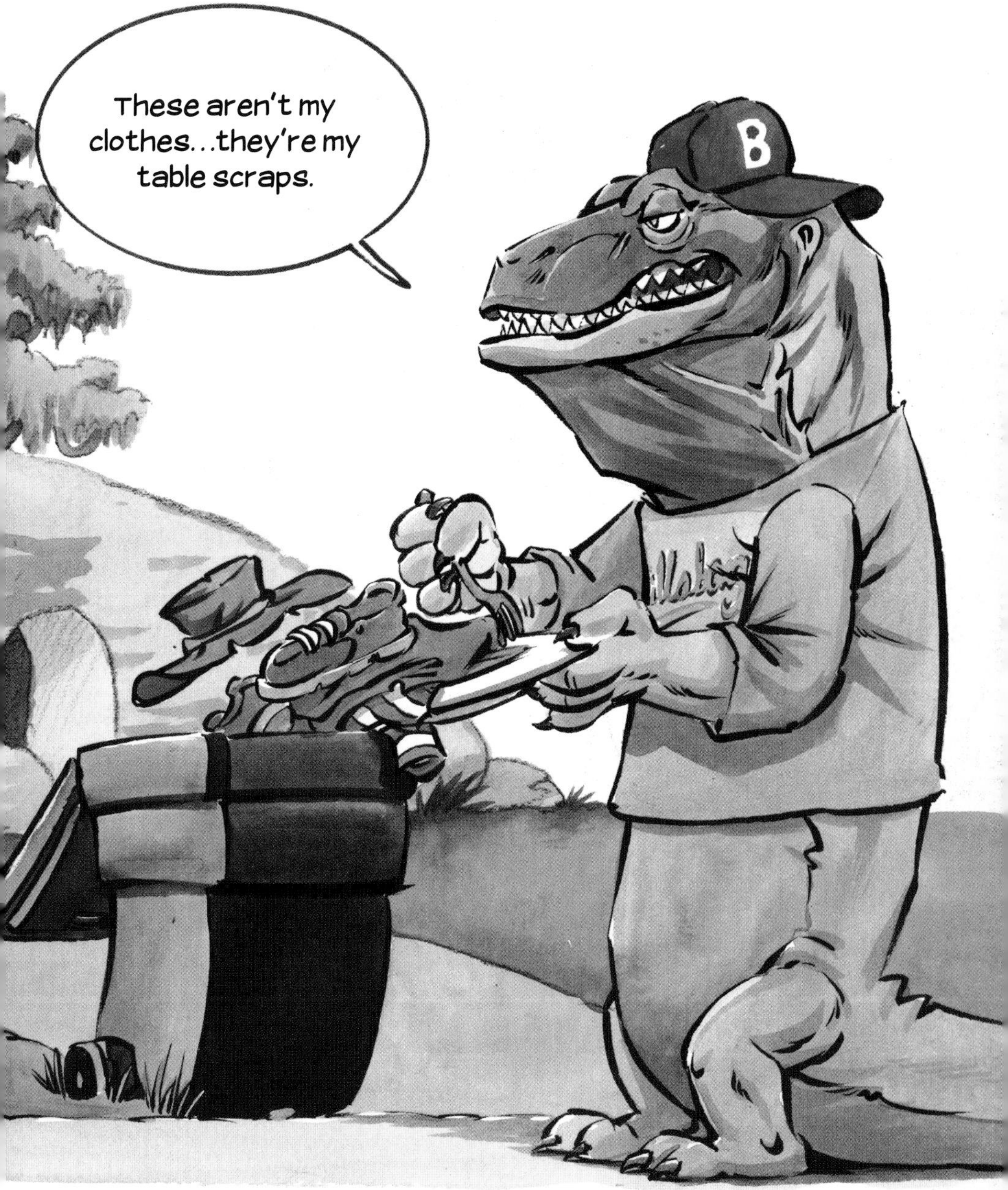
These aren't my clothes...they're my table scraps.
B

The Komodo dragon eats the bones, hooves and fur of its victims. Only 12% of its prey will not be consumed, which is a much lower percentage compared to the lion, which leaves behind 25 to 30% of its meal.

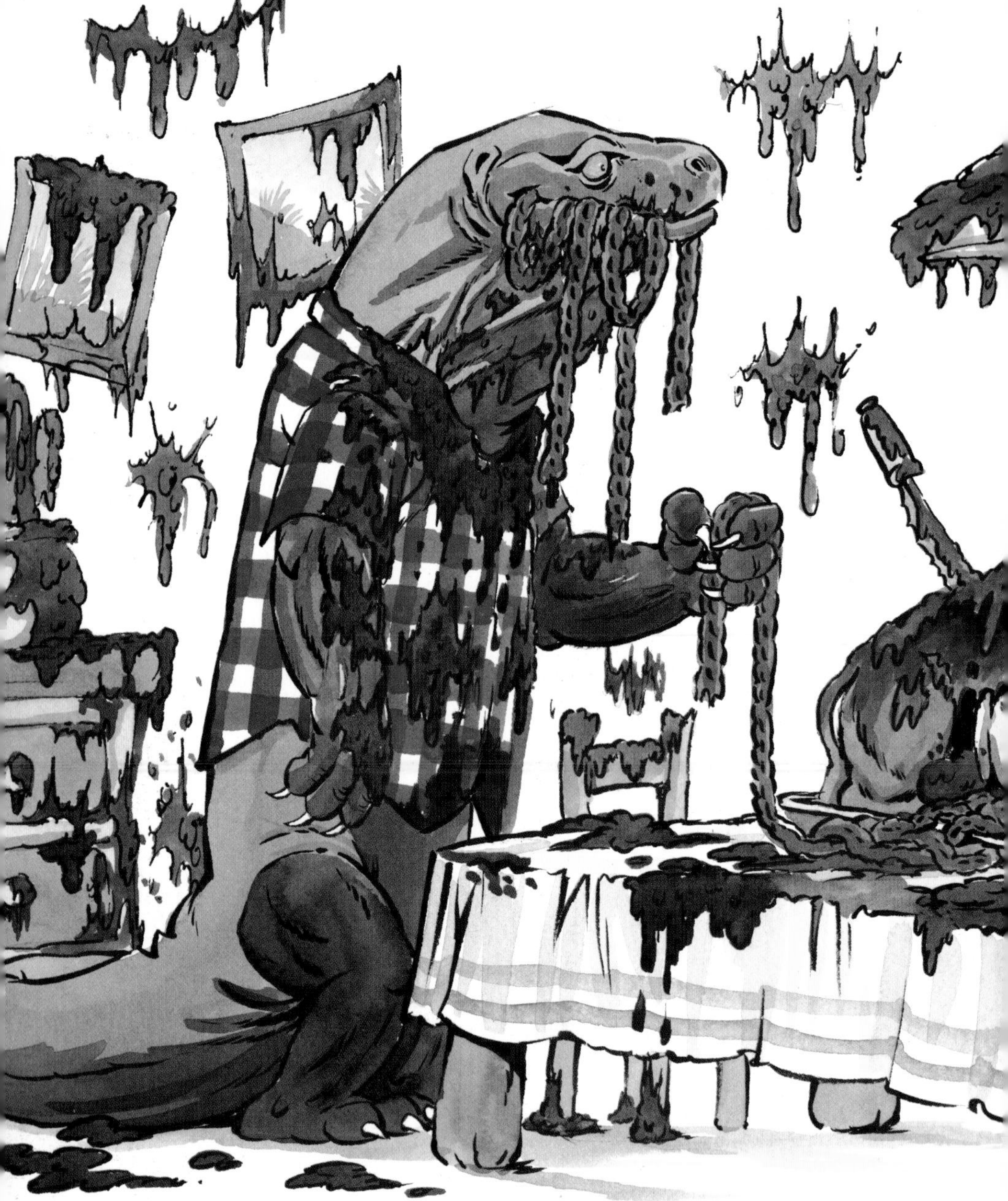

The Komodo dragon will vigorously shake its prey's intestines to void them of their contents before eating them.

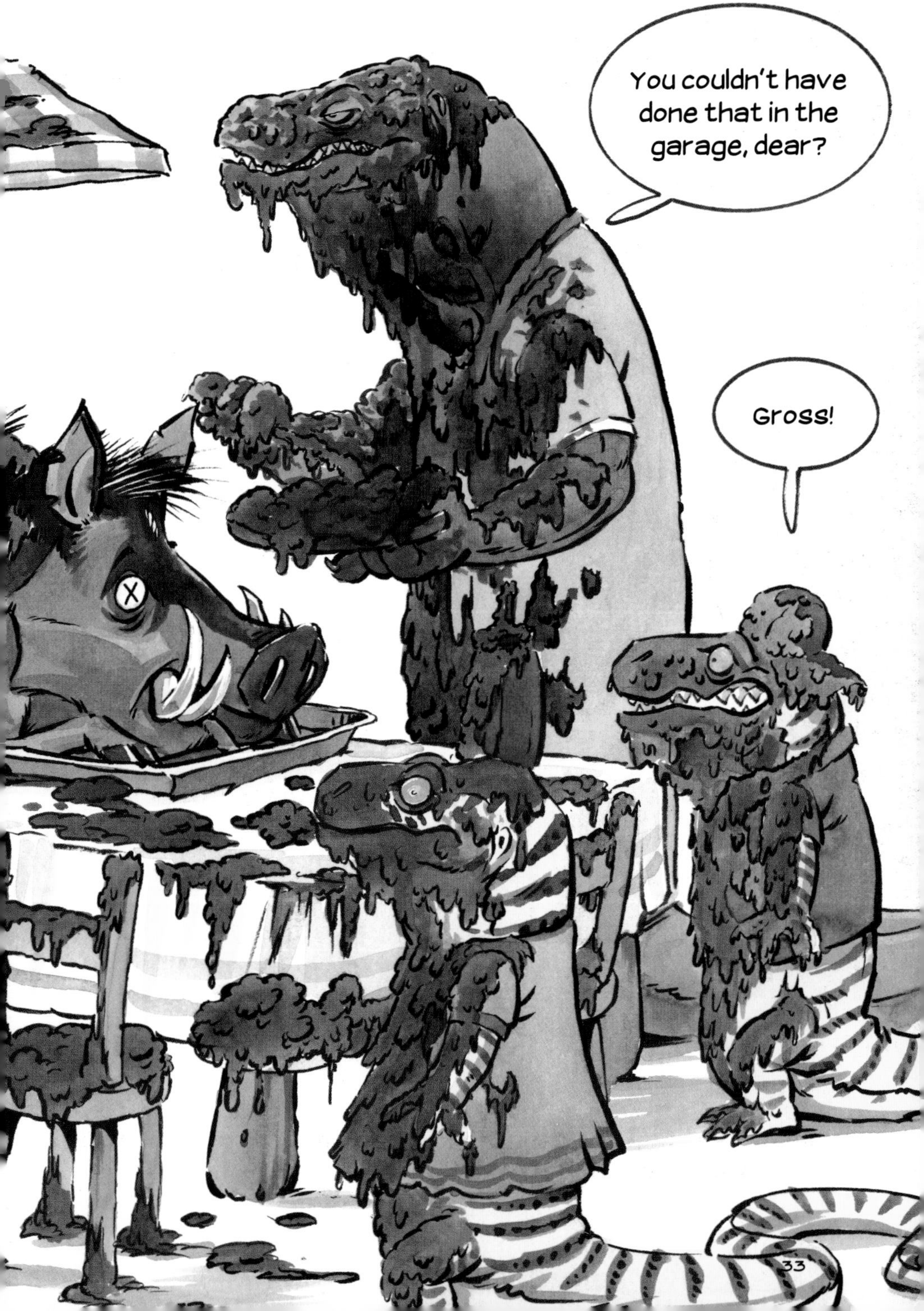
You couldn't have done that in the garage, dear?
Gross!

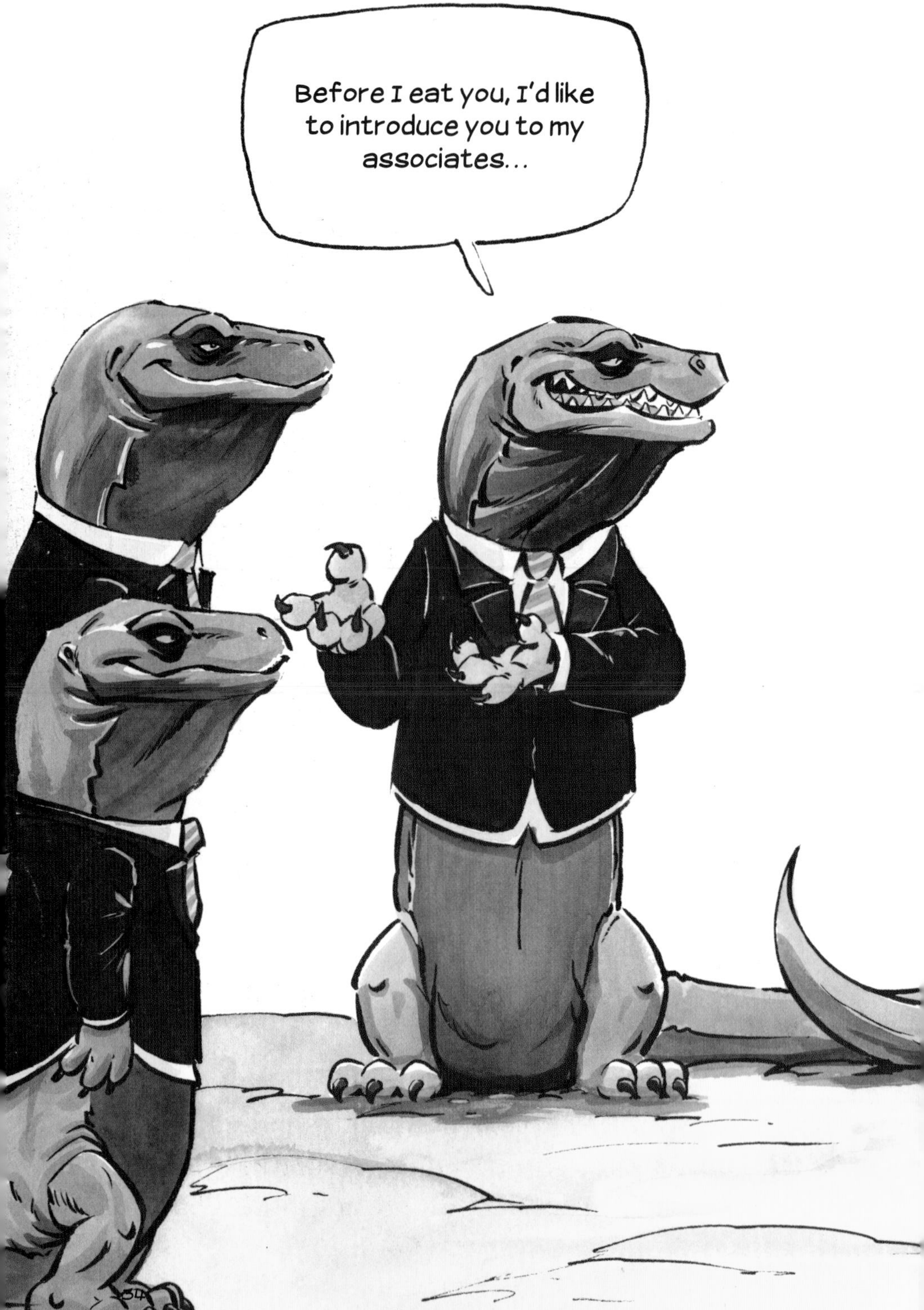
Before I eat you, I'd like to introduce you to my associates...

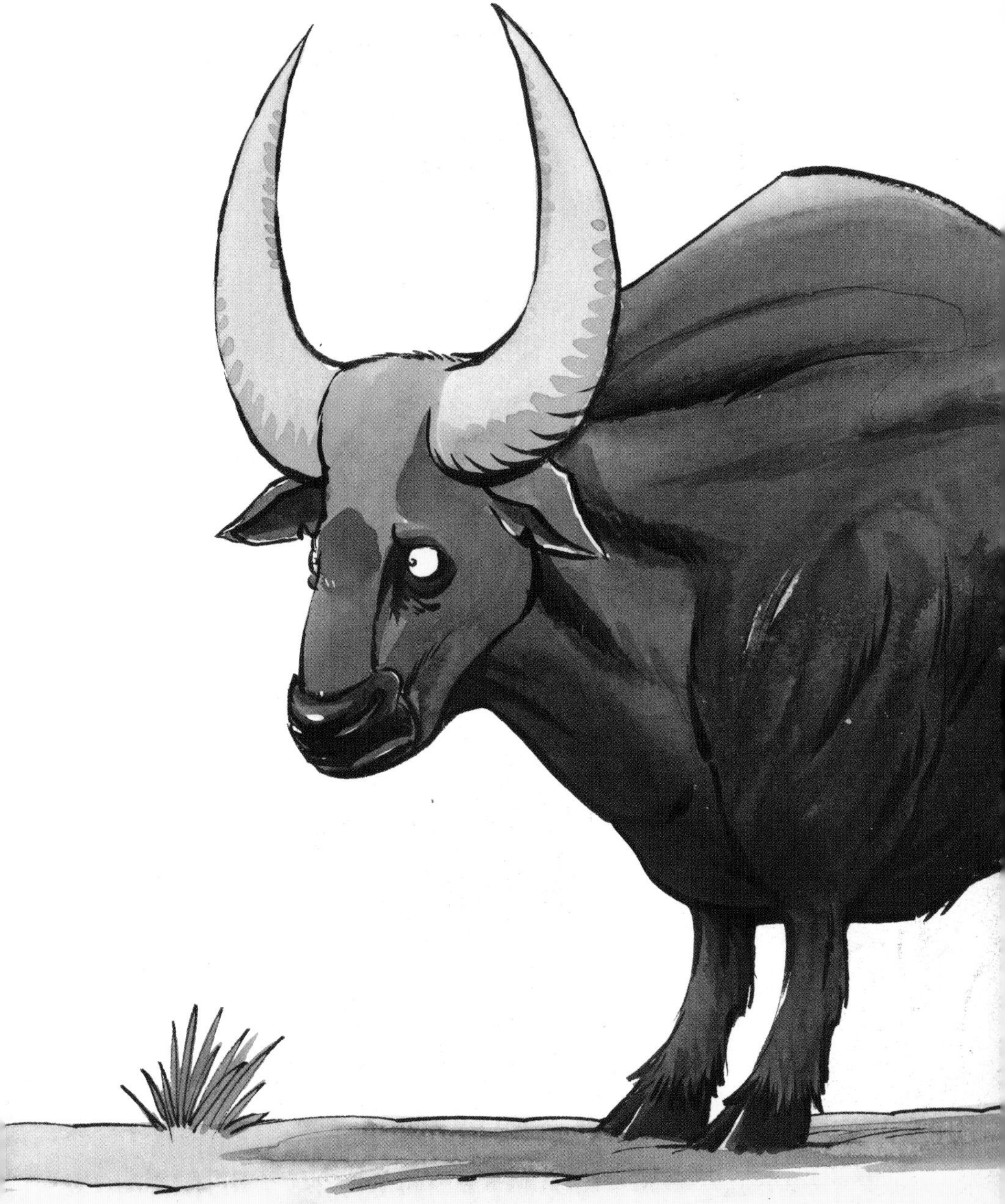

Komodo dragons have been known to gang up to kill larger animals. However, the largest males will have priority feeding once they start eating.

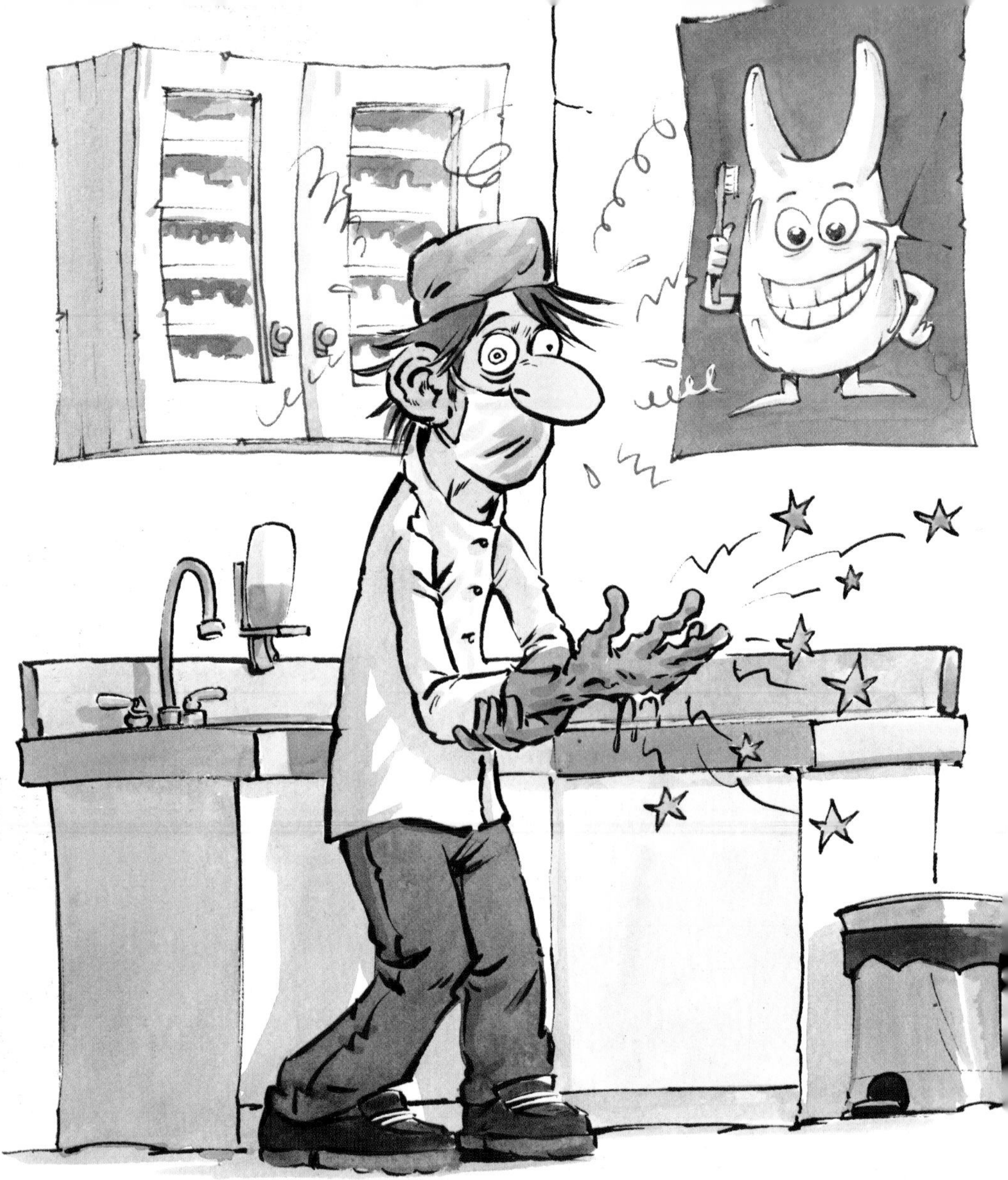

An injury from a Komodo dragon bite will always lead to an infection. If an injured animal escapes, it will die from blood poisoning shortly afterward.

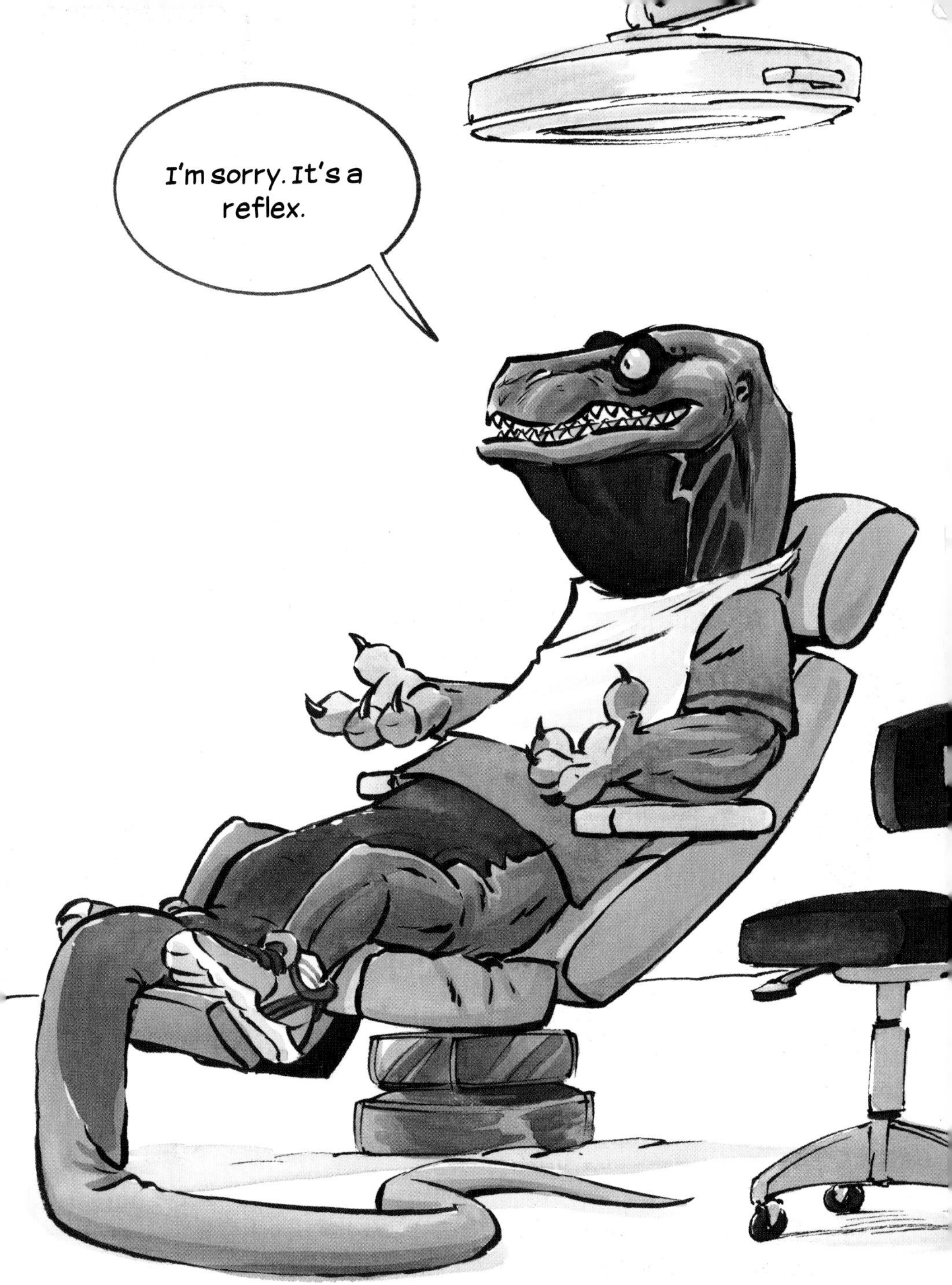
I'm sorry. It's a reflex.

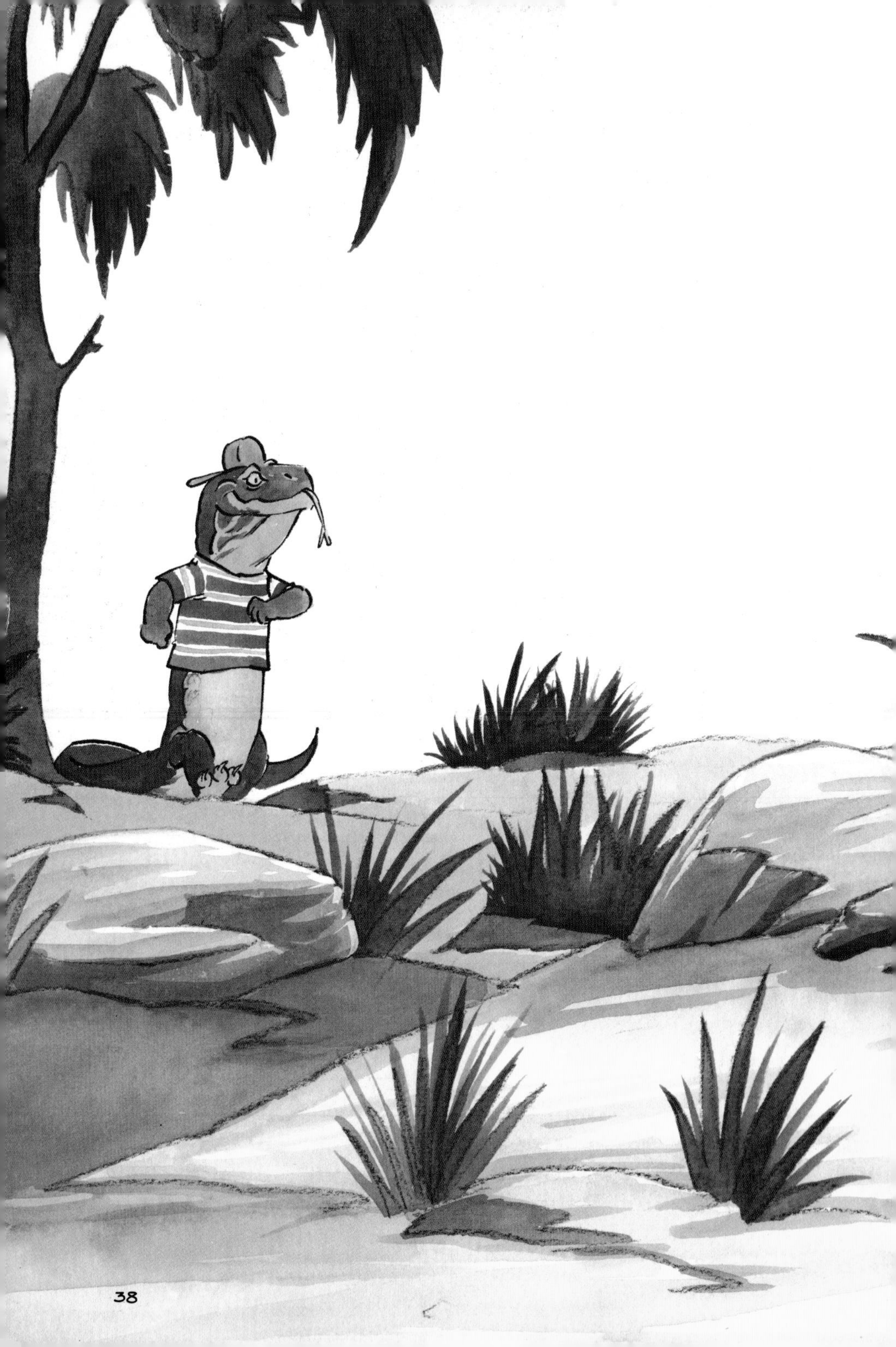

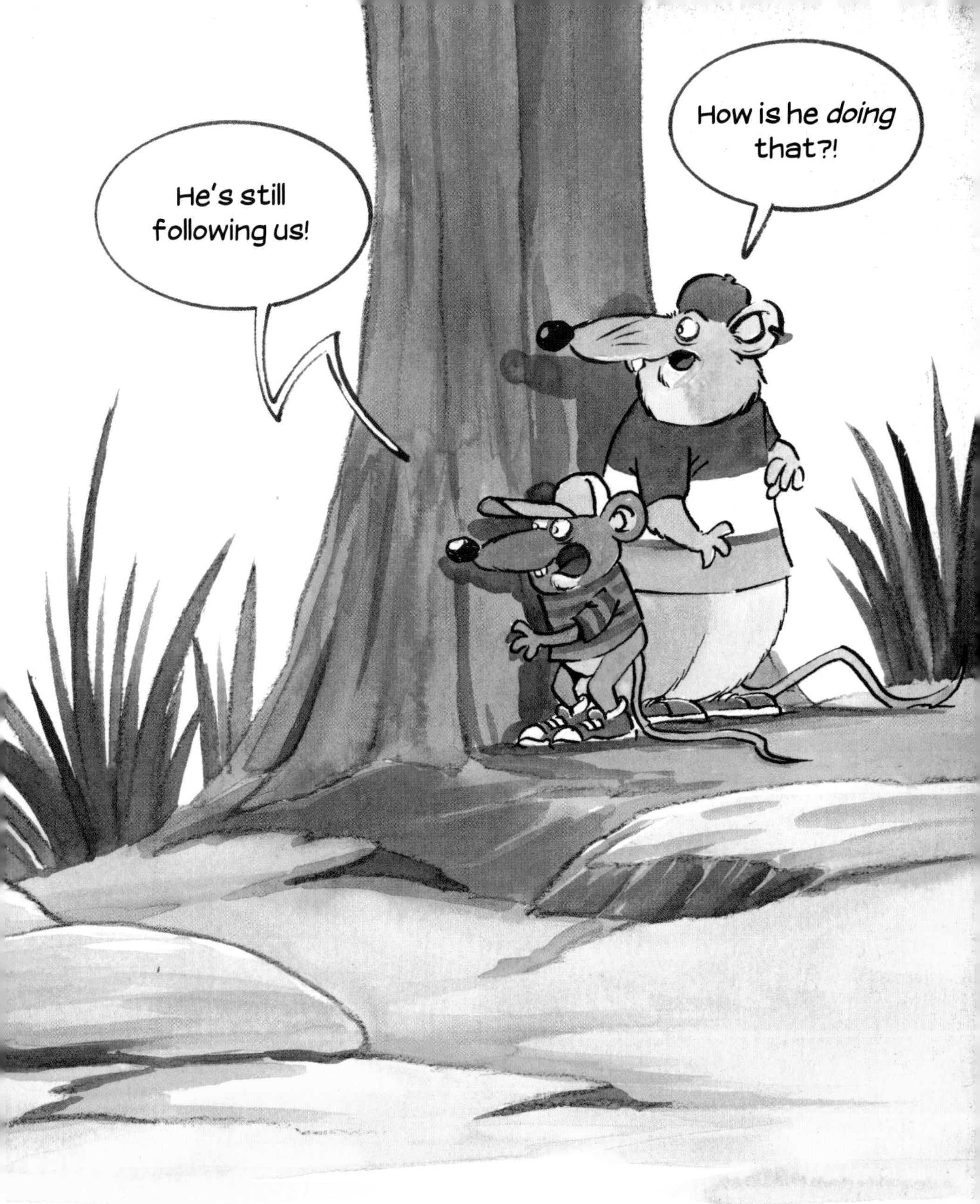
He's still following us!
How is he *doing* that?!

The Komodo dragon's extraordinary sense of smell allows it to follow the trace of its prey from several kilometres away.

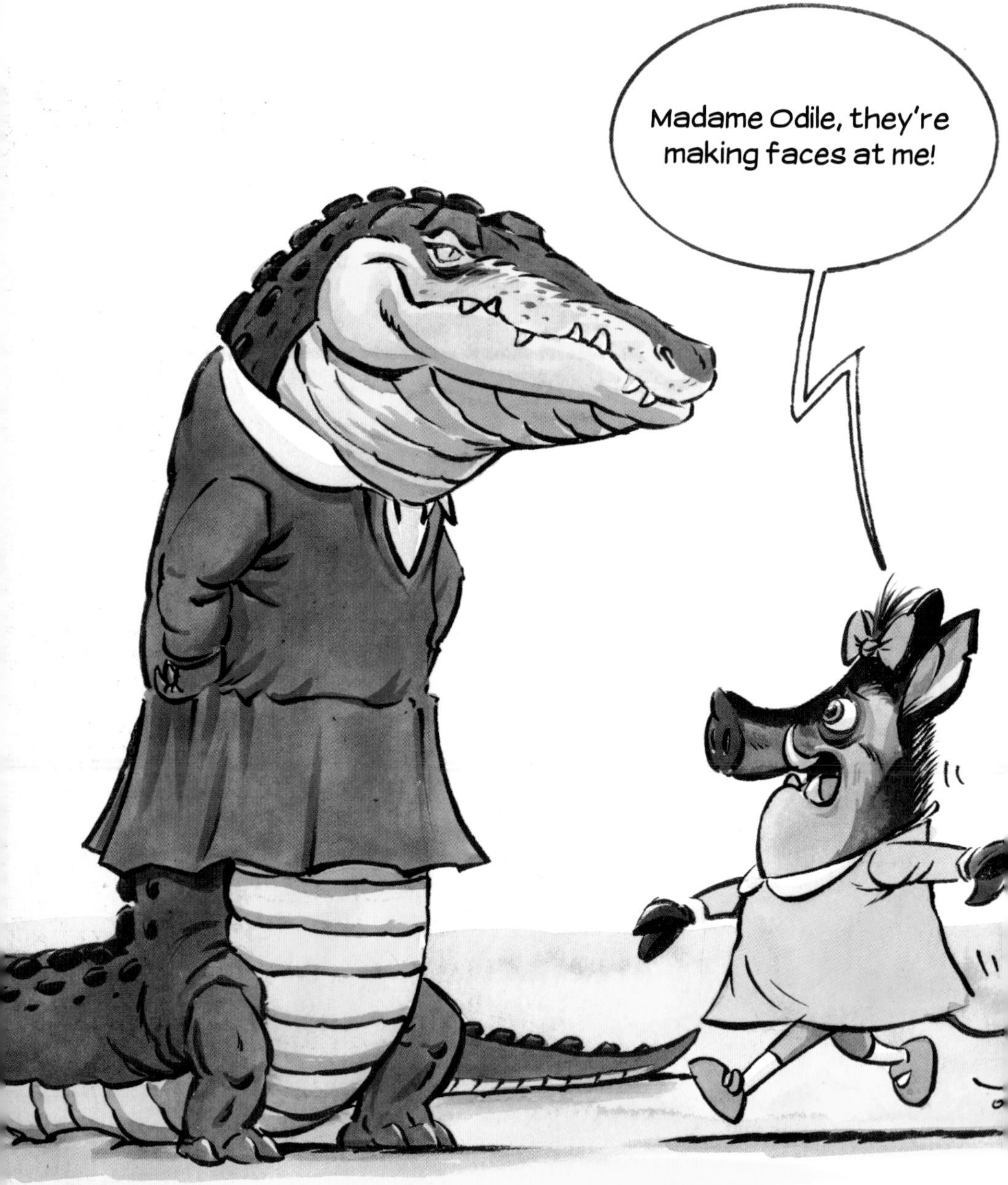
Madame Odile, they're making faces at me!

The Komodo dragon constantly sticks out its long, forked tongue in order to collect odour molecules in the air.

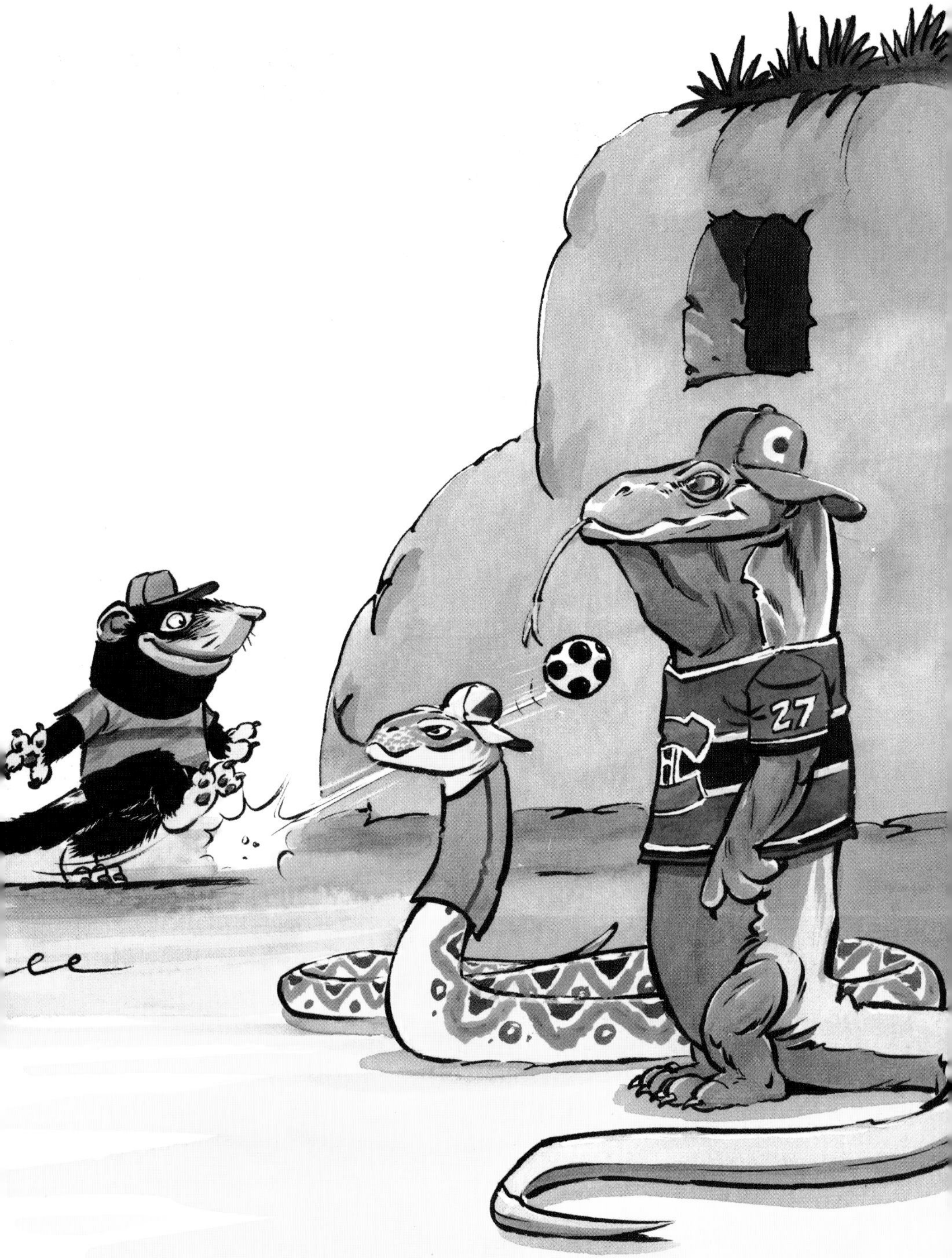
27

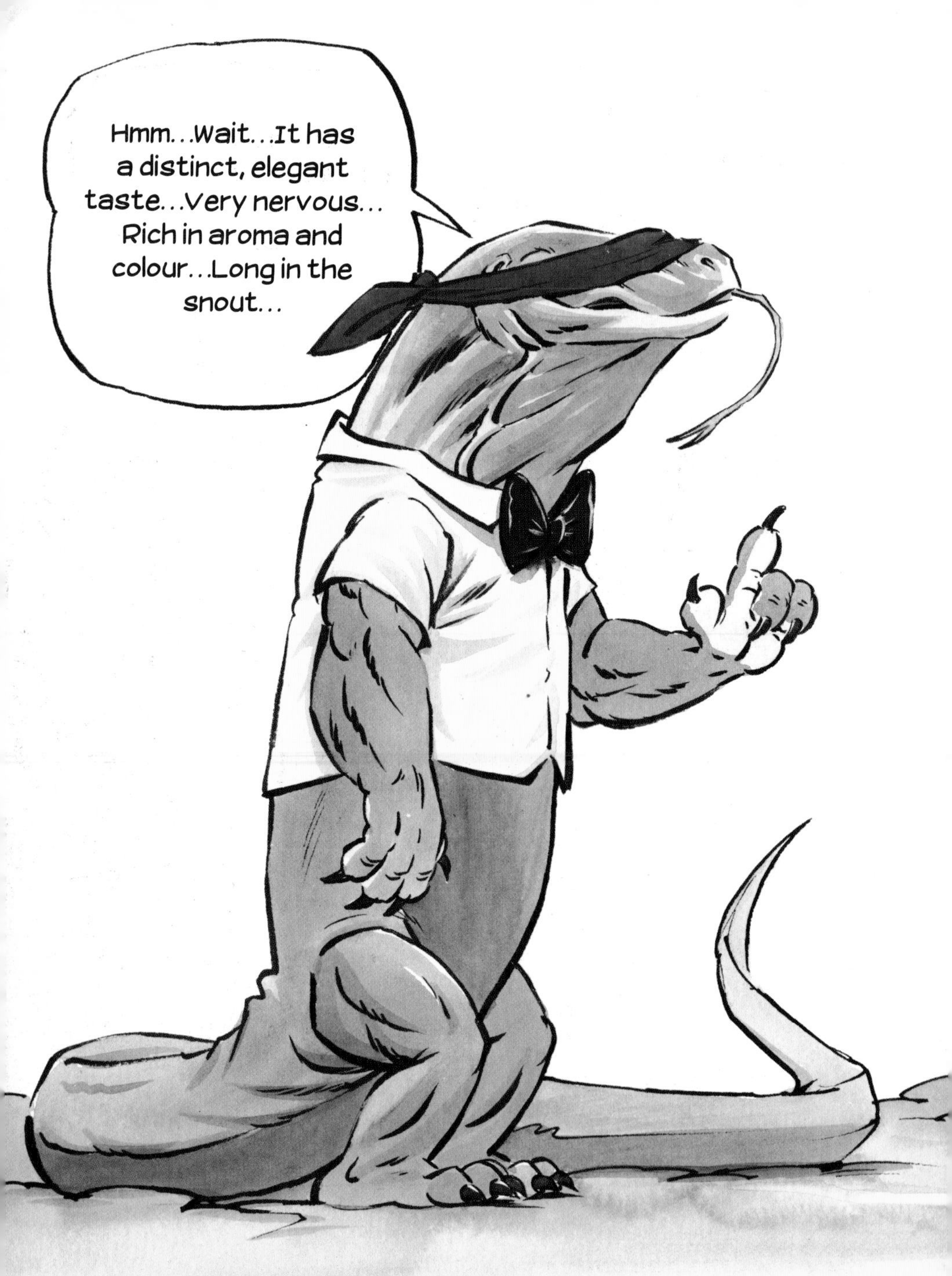
Hmm...Wait...It has a distinct, elegant taste...Very nervous... Rich in aroma and colour...Long in the snout...

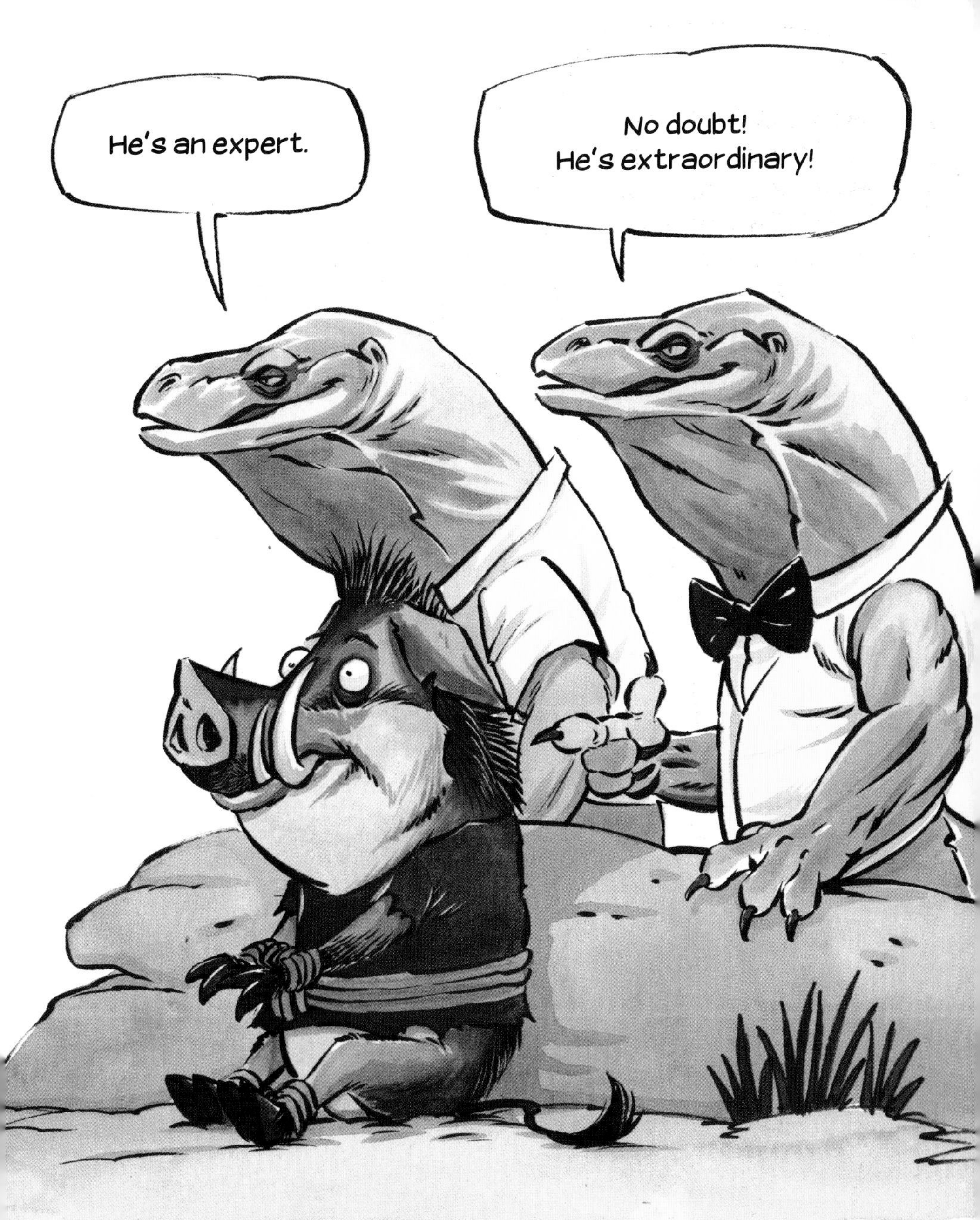
He's an expert.
No doubt!
He's extraordinary!

Komodo dragons can taste the odours released from their future prey by licking air particles and analyzing them.

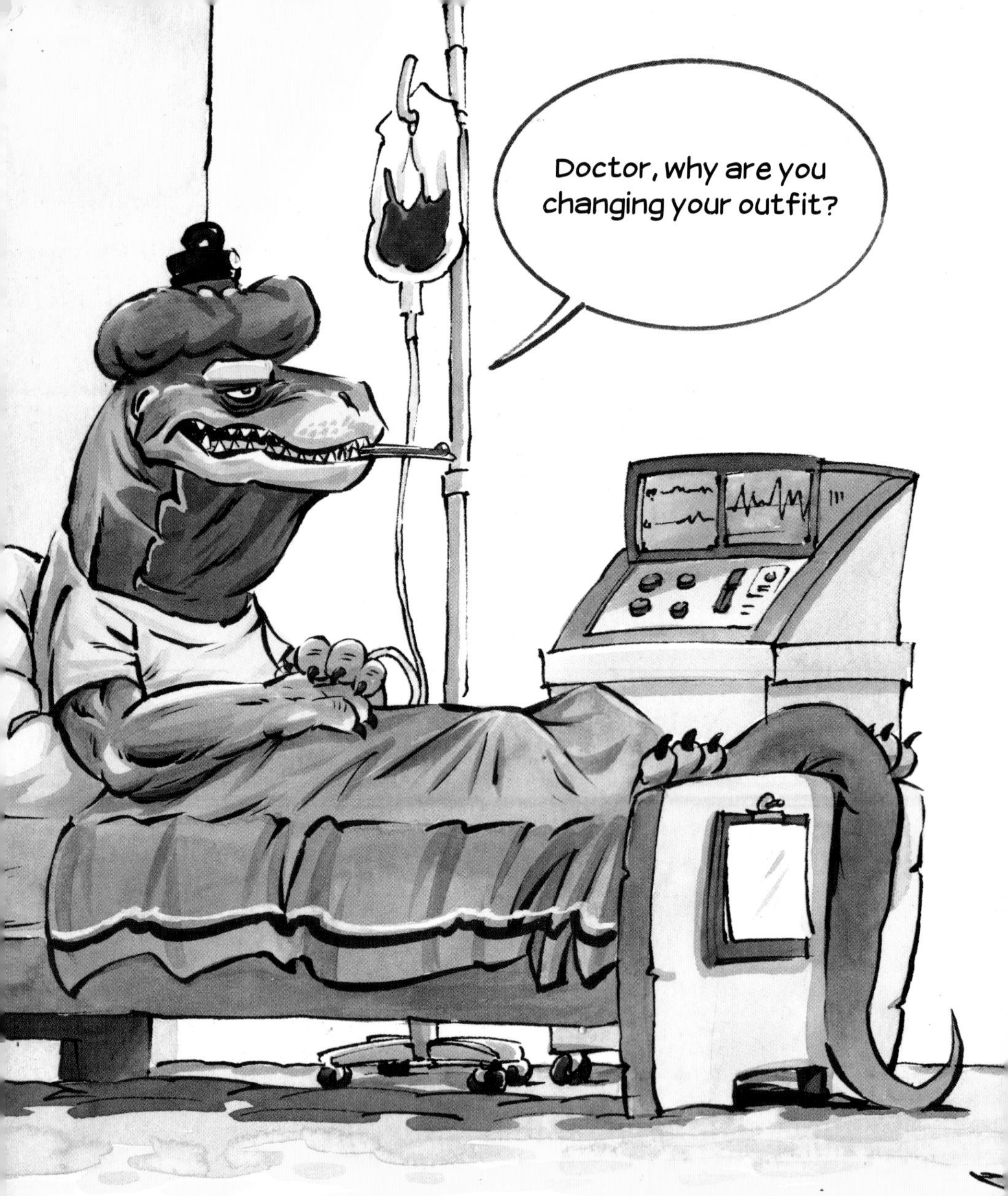
Doctor, why are you changing your outfit?

Cannibalism is one of the main causes of death in Komodo dragons.

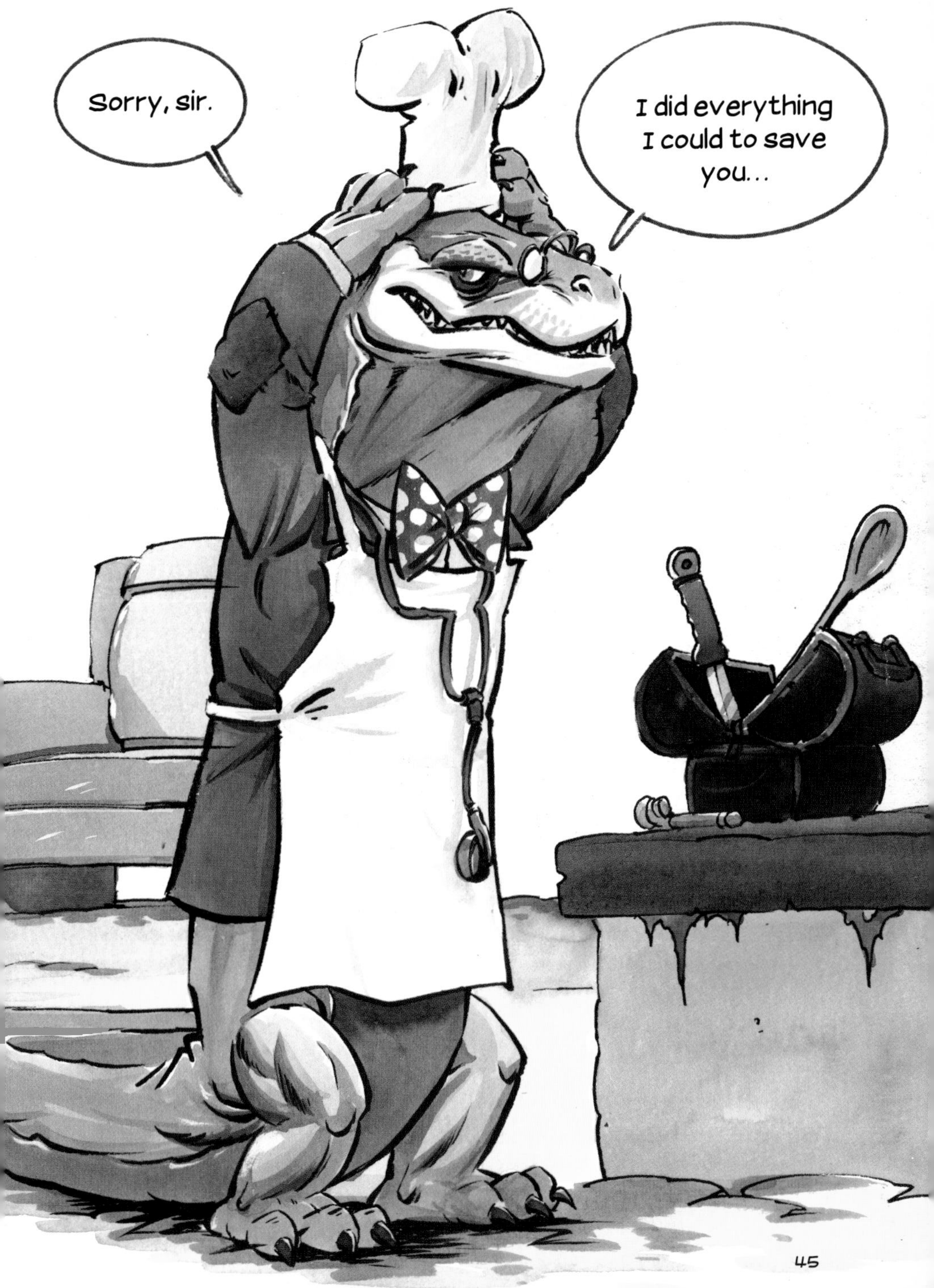
Sorry, sir.
I did everything I could to save you...

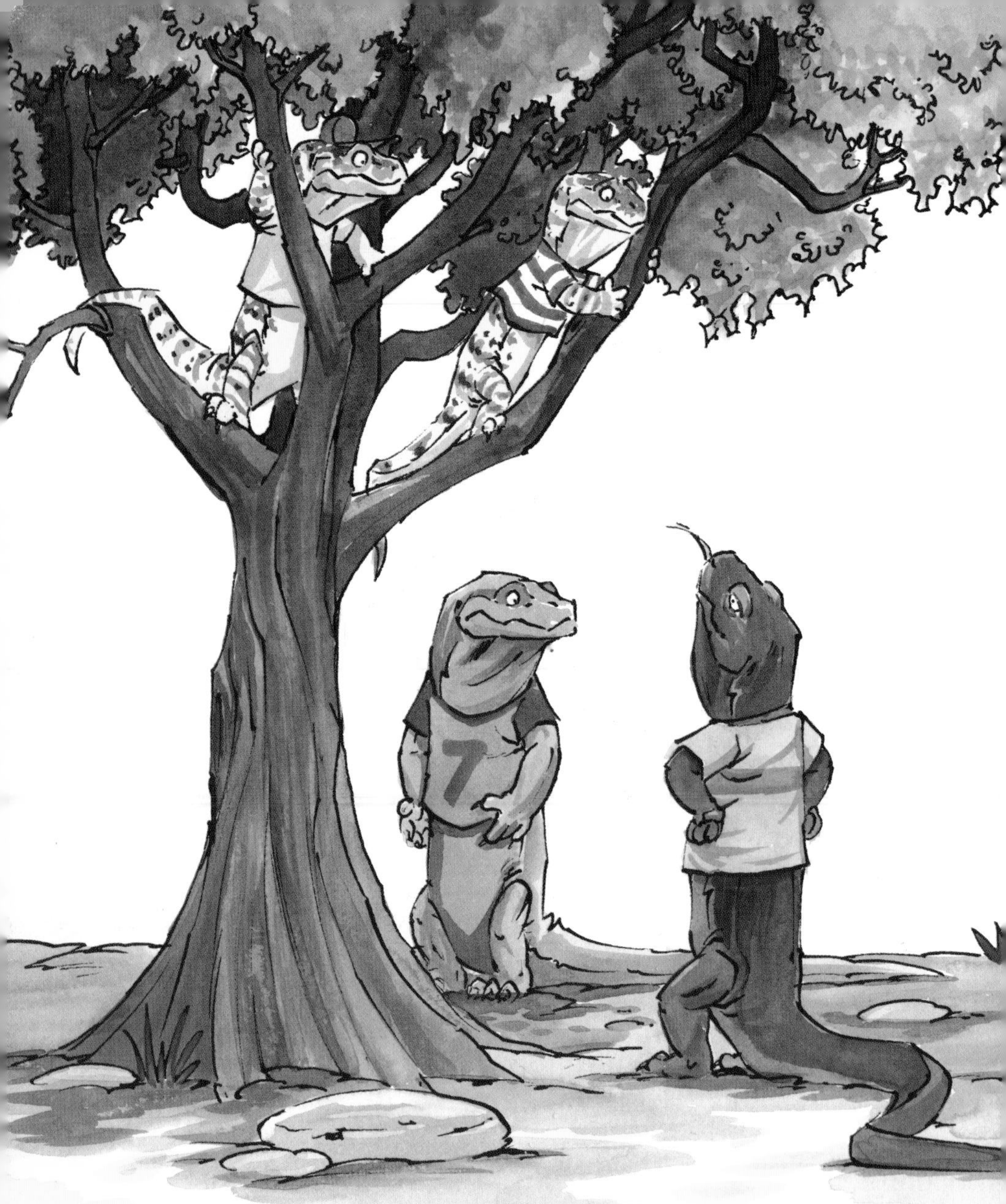

During their first few years, young Komodo dragons must take shelter in trees in order to escape the cannibalism of their elders. They are safe high up in the trees because adult Komodo dragons cannot climb.

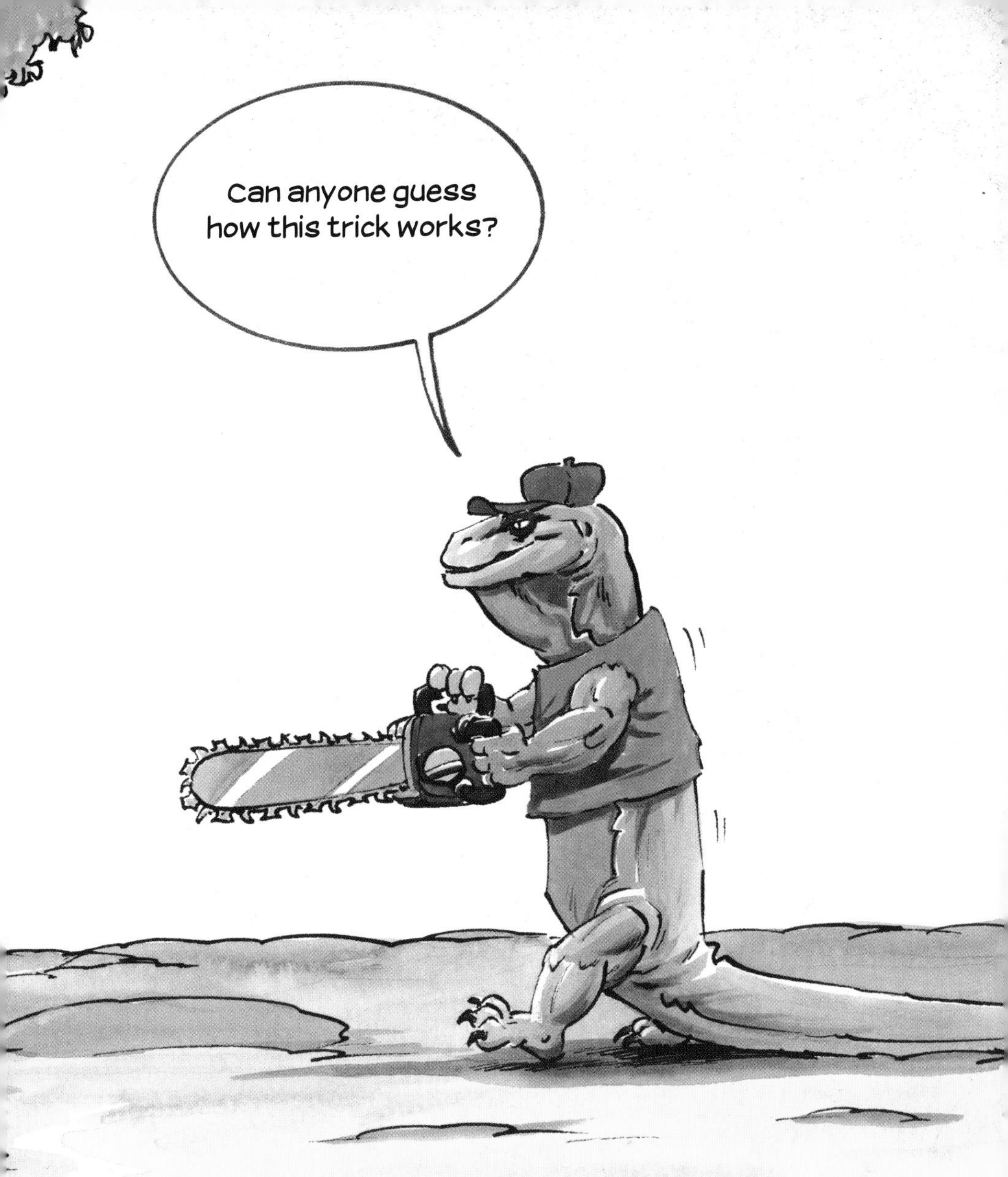
Can anyone guess how this trick works?

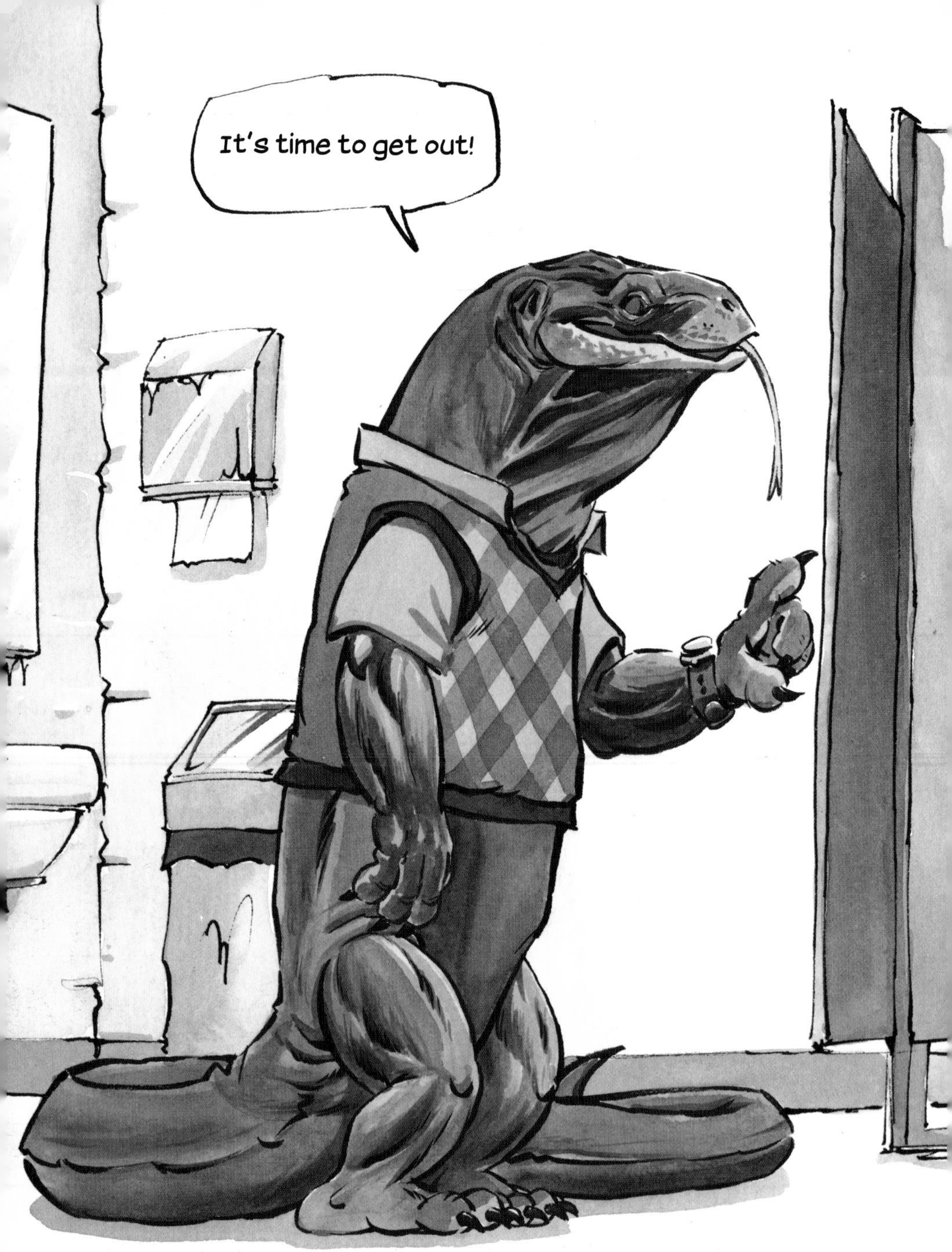
It's time to get out!

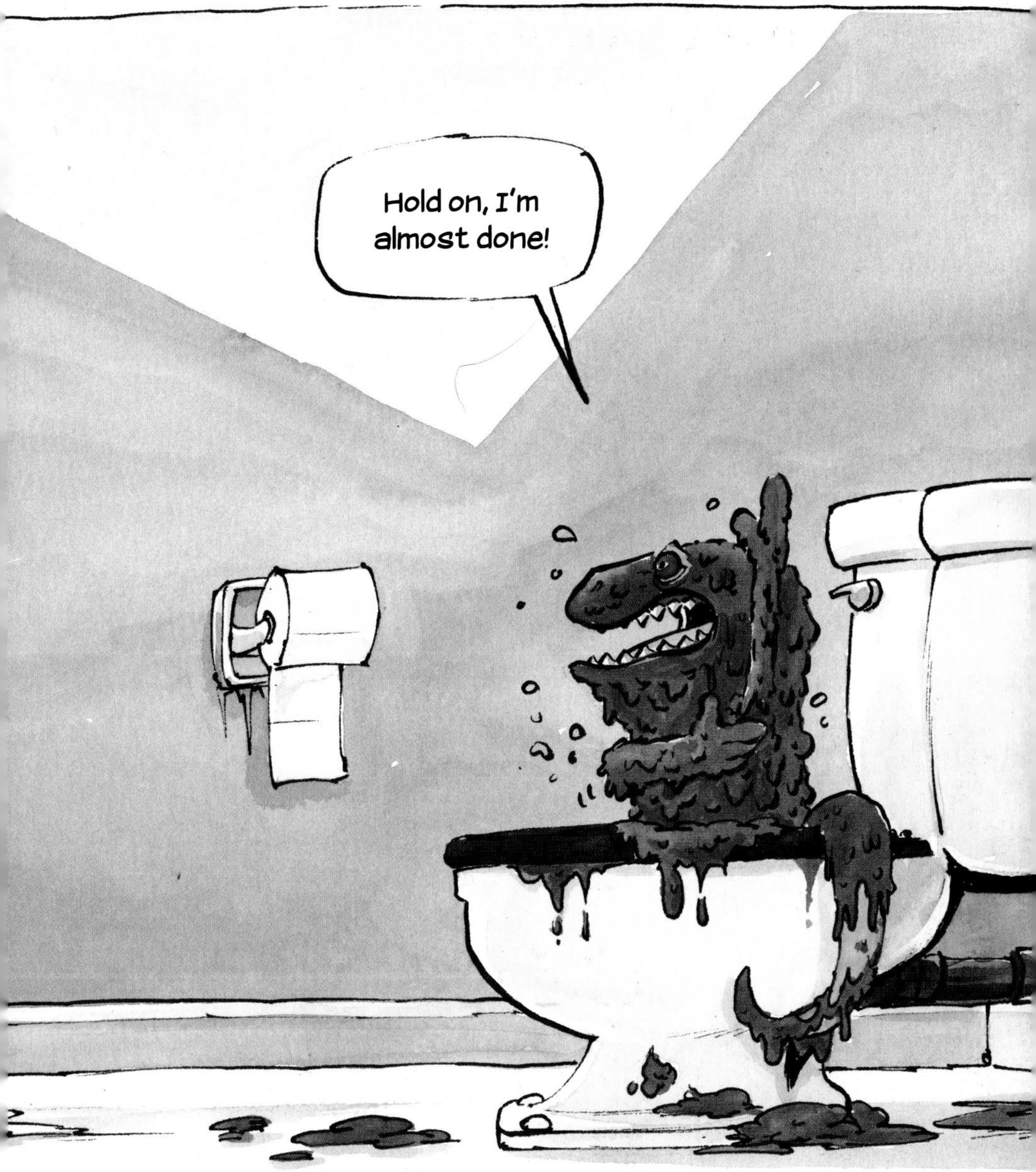
Hold on, I'm almost done!

Young Komodo dragons will also roll around in excrement in order to avoid being eaten by their elders.

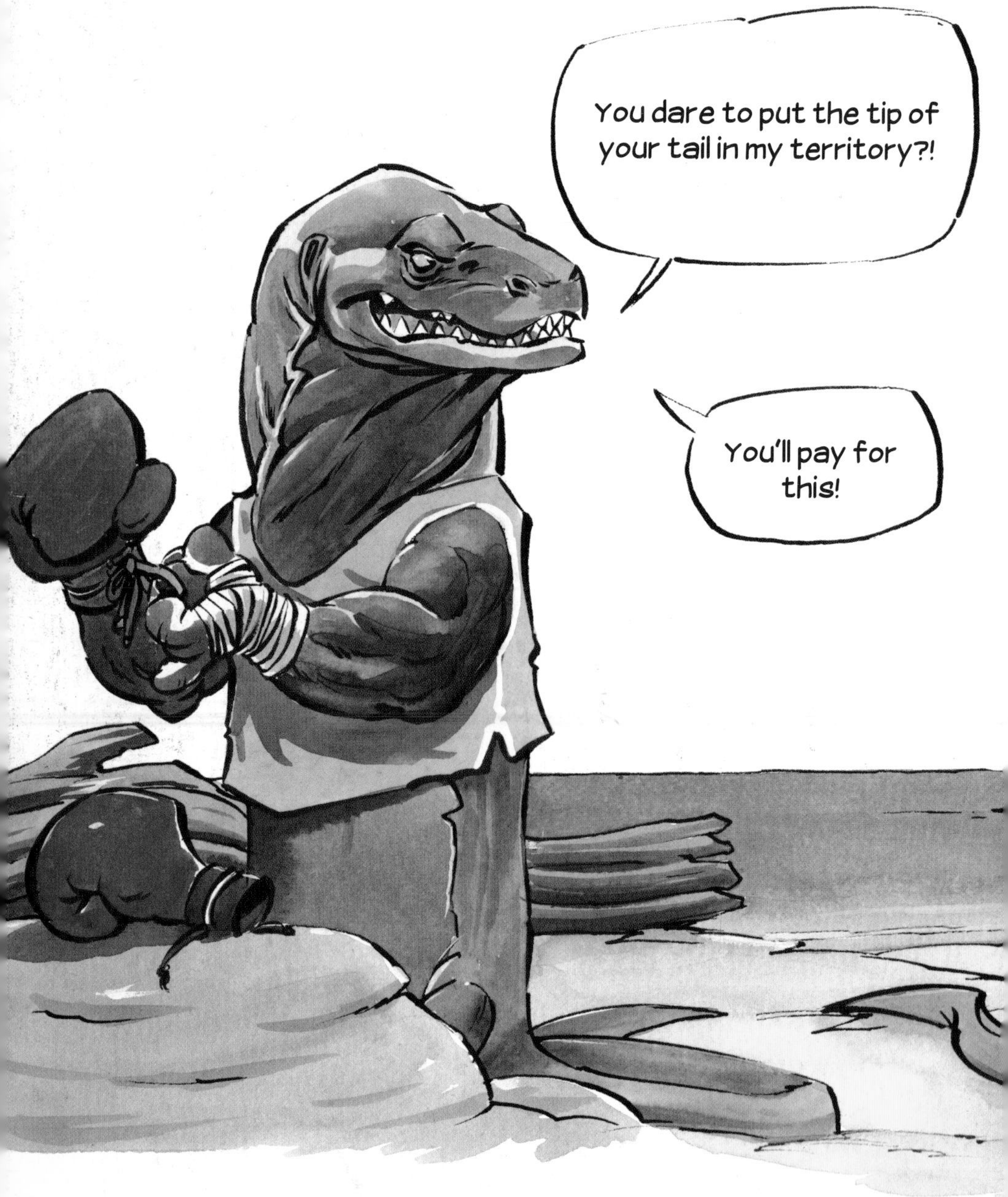
You dare to put the tip of your tail in my territory?!
You'll pay for this!

Komodo dragons are **solitary** and extremely **territorial**. They are aggressive and are not afraid of fighting to defend their territory.

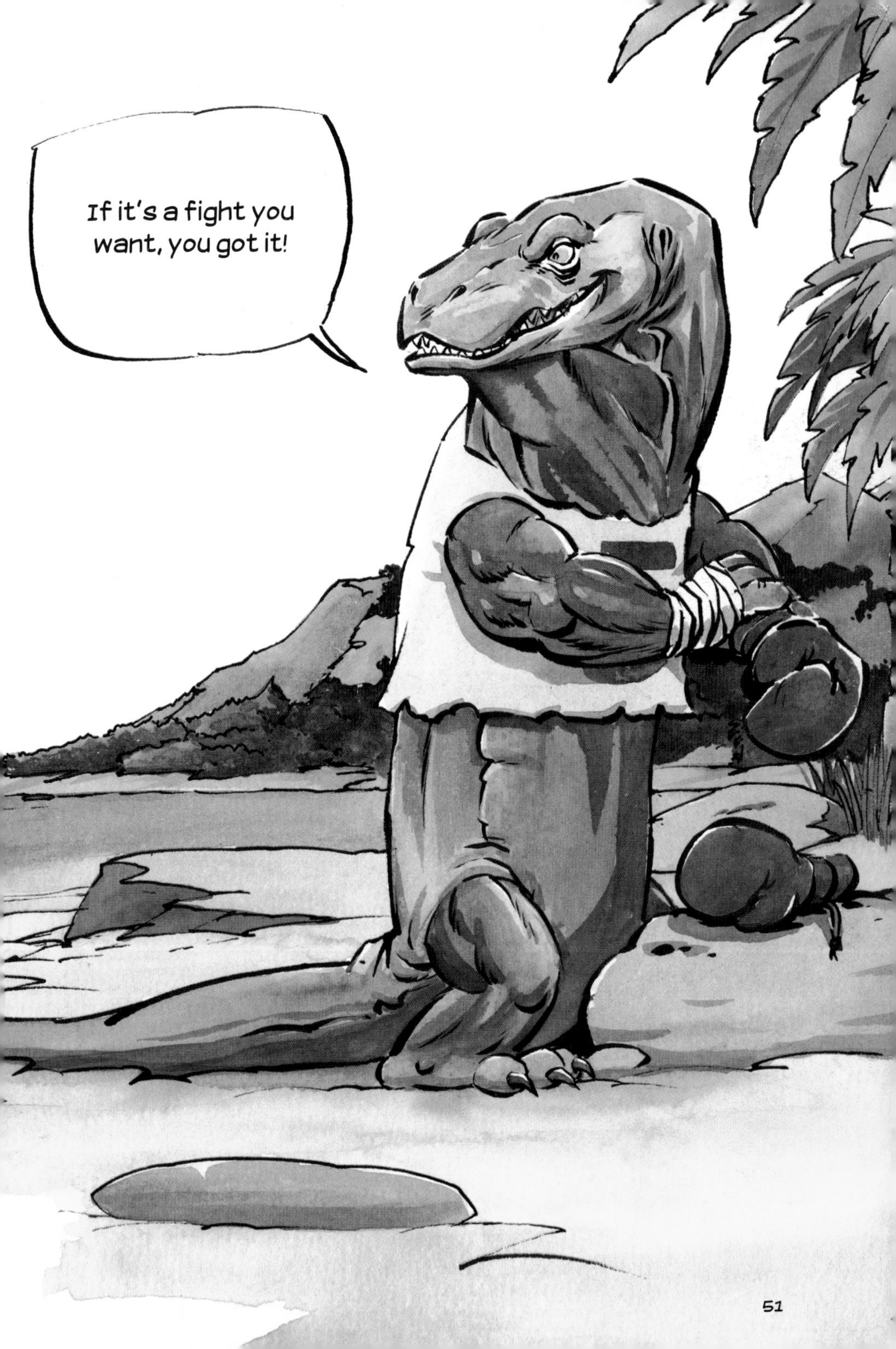
If it's a fight you want, you got it!

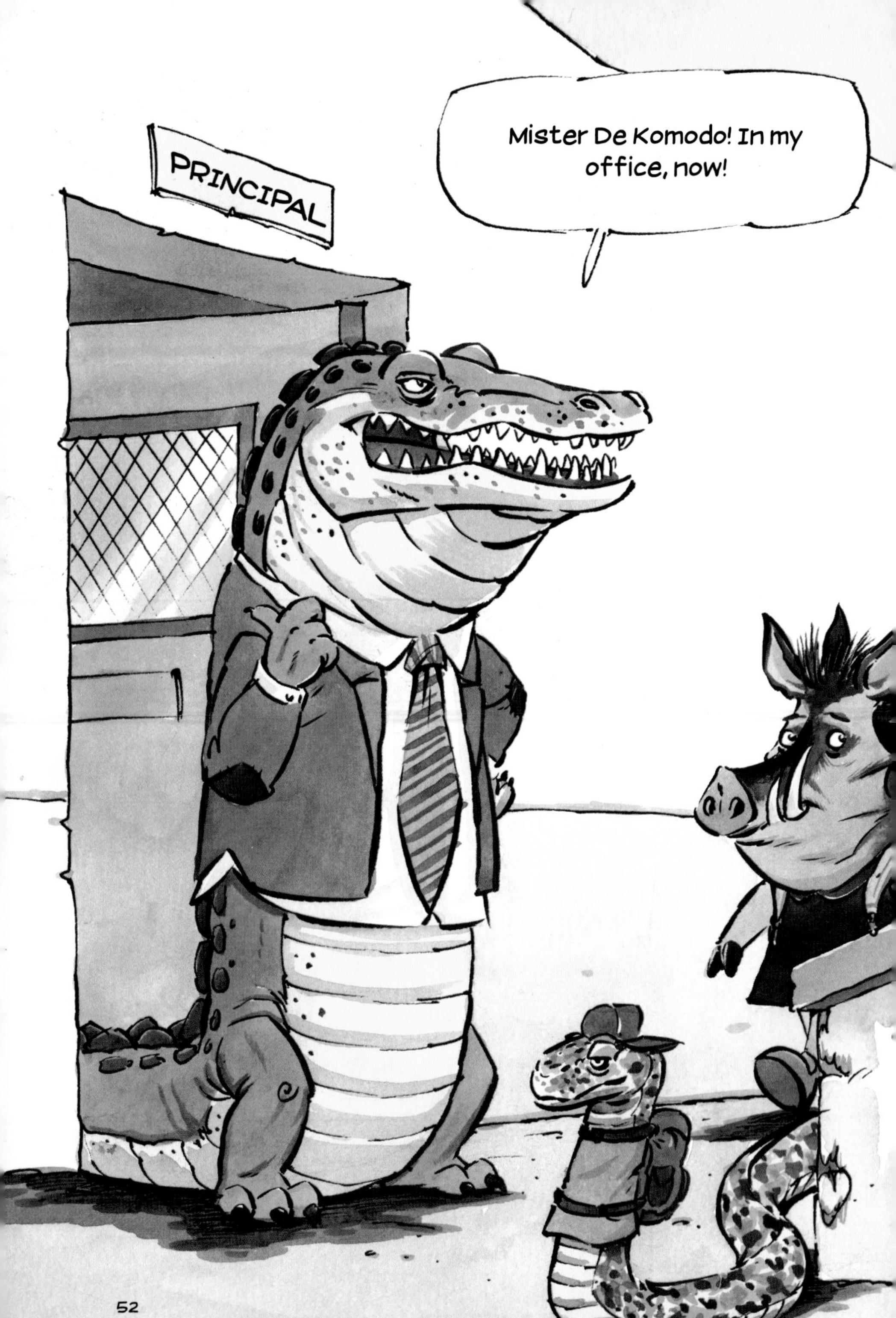
PRINCIPAL
Mister De Komodo! In my office, now!

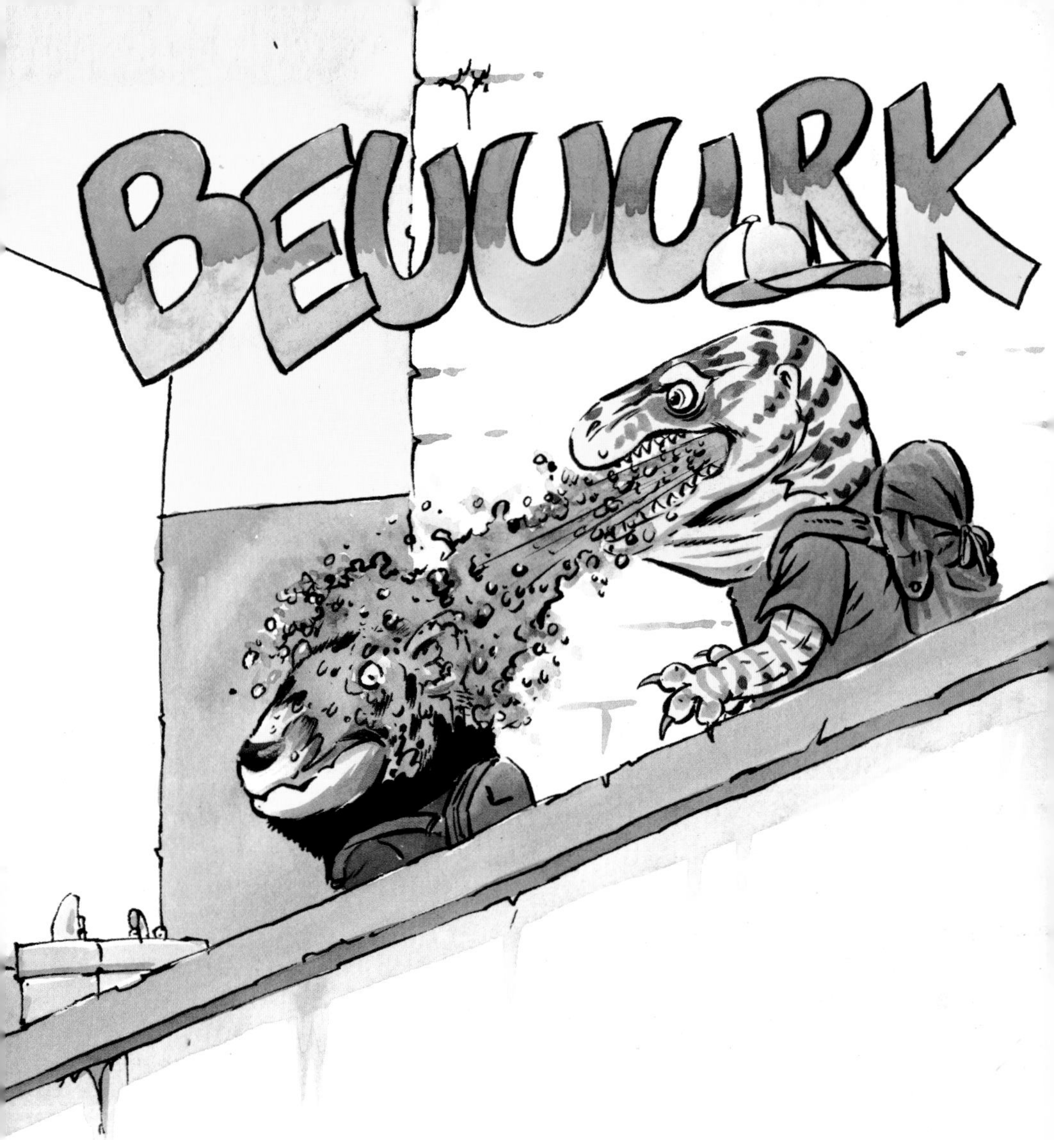
BEUUURK

If they feel threatened, Komodo dragons can reduce their body weight by vomiting the contents of their stomachs in order to escape more quickly with a lighter weight.

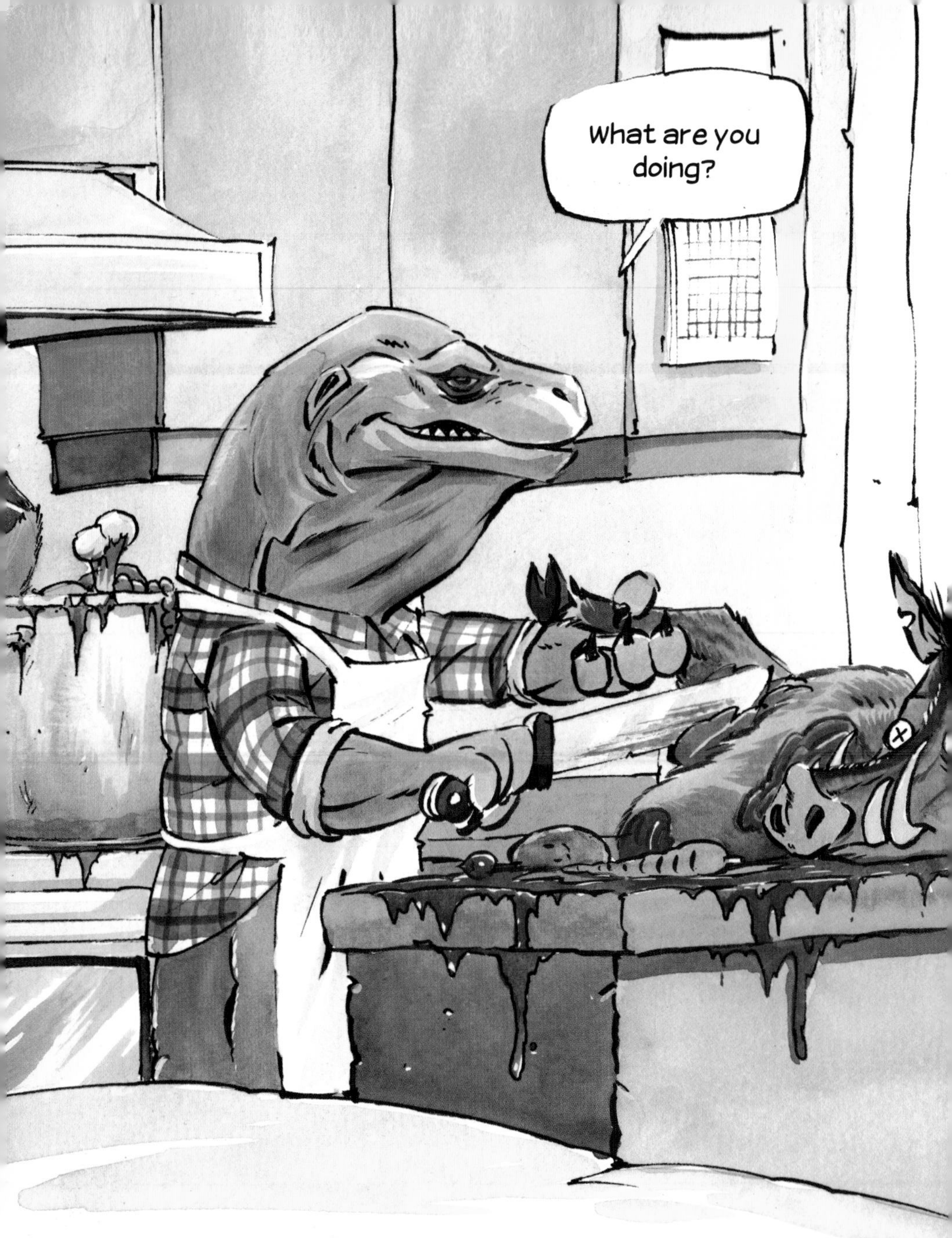
What are you doing?

Komodo dragons reach sexual maturity at 6 years of age. The female can lay up to 40 eggs.

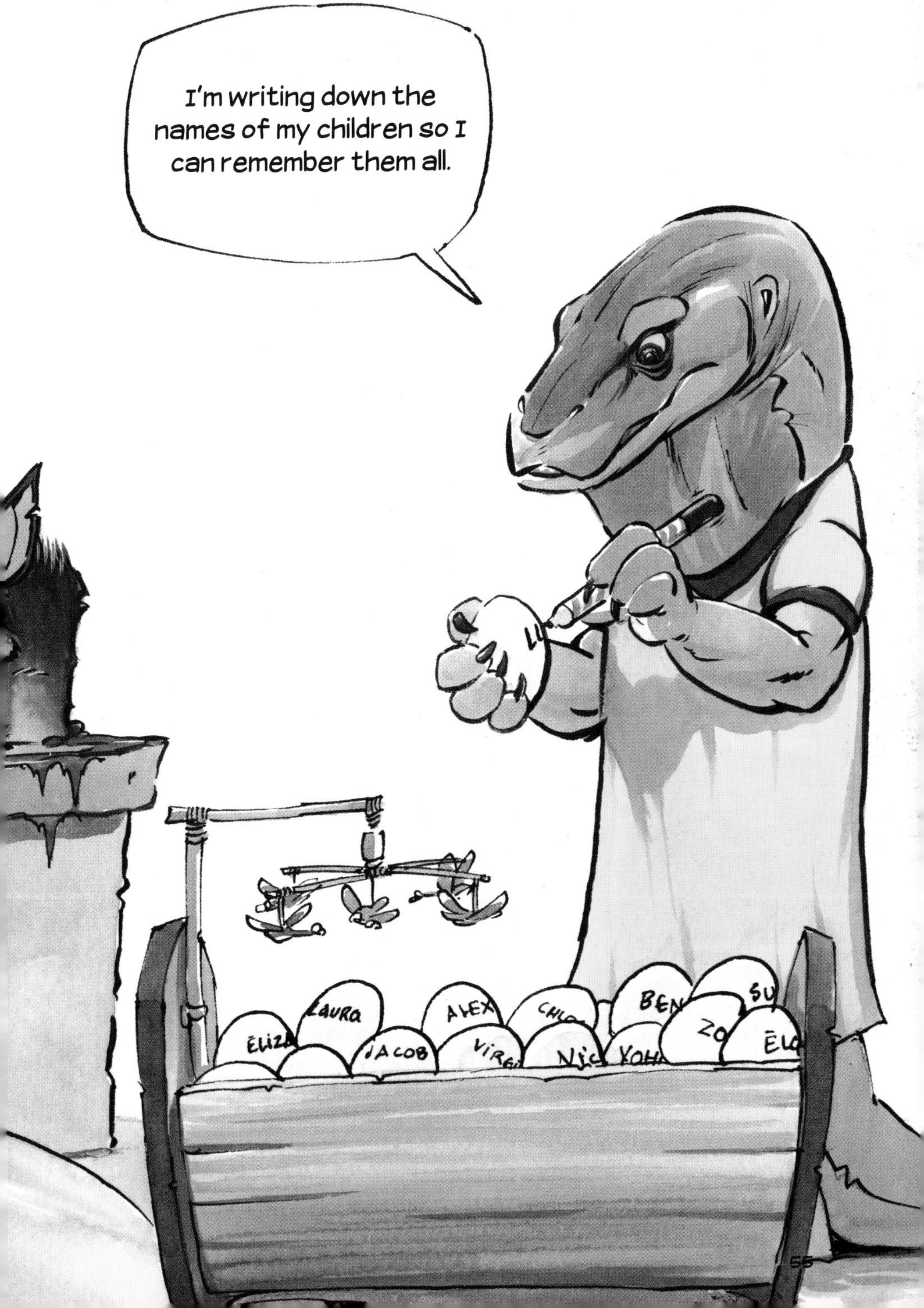
I'm writing down the names of my children so I can remember them all.
LAURA
ALEX
ELIZA
JACOB
BEN

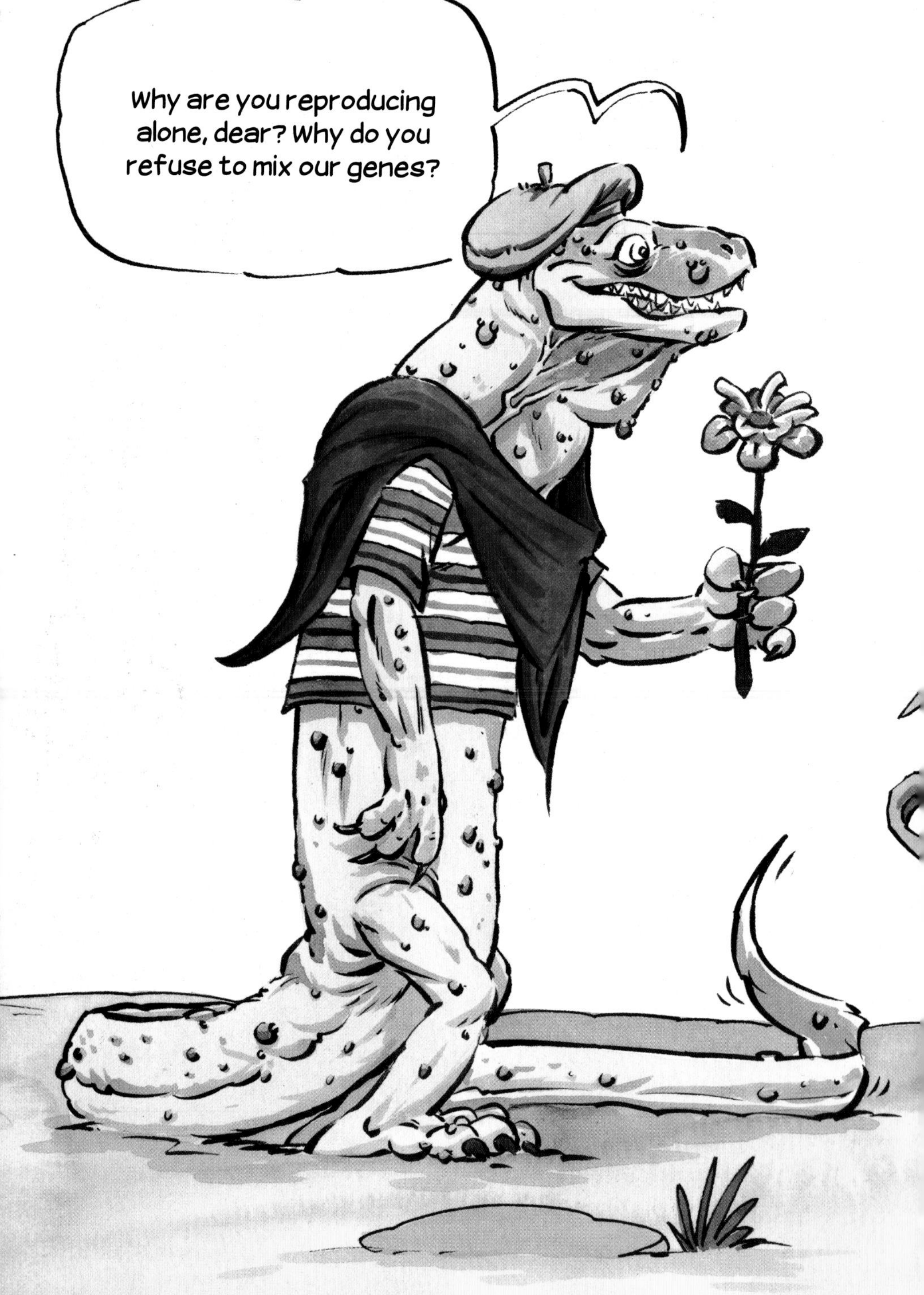
Why are you reproducing alone, dear? Why do you refuse to mix our genes?

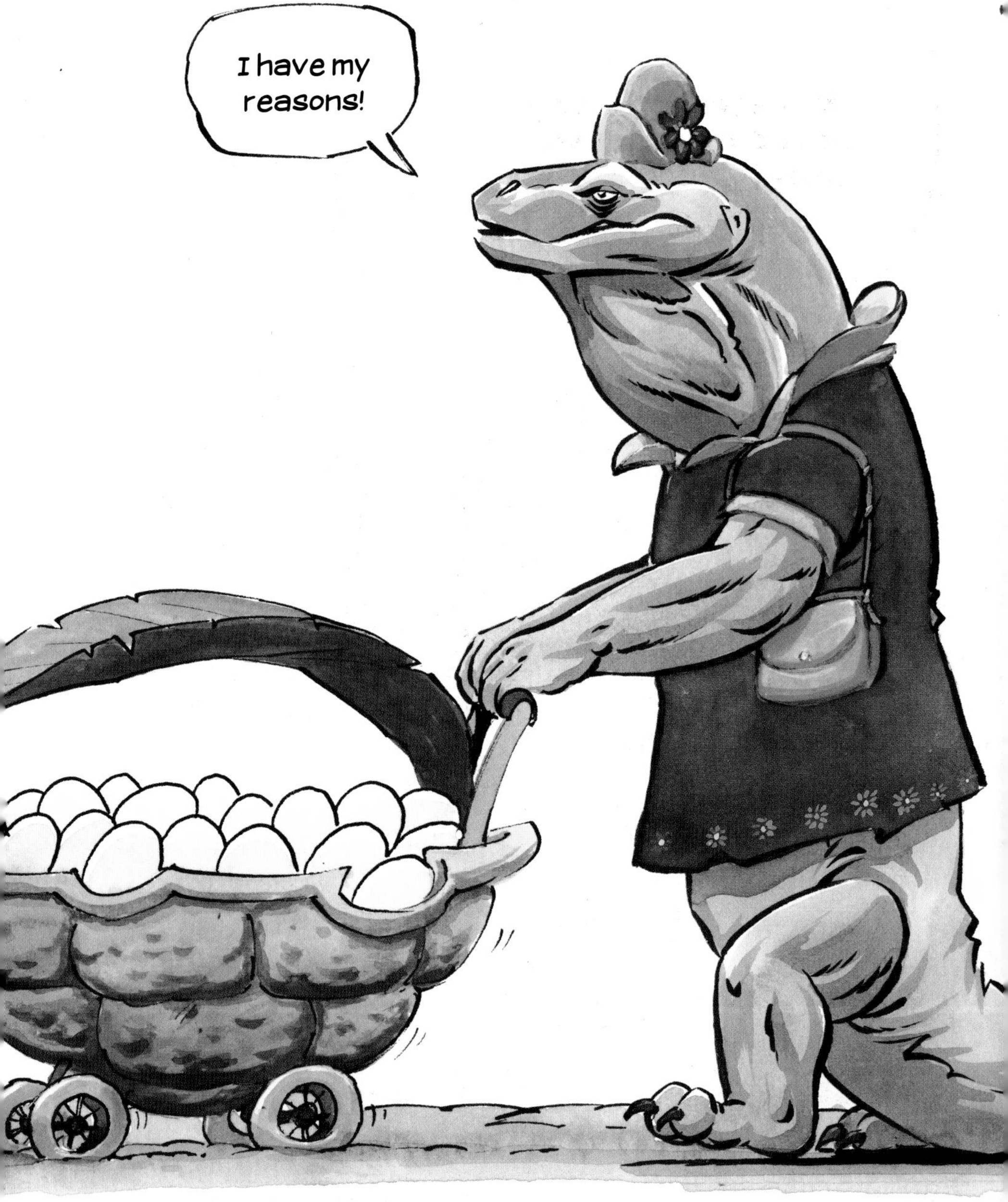
I have my reasons!

In addition to reproducing sexually with a mate, the female Komodo dragon can also produce clones by herself.

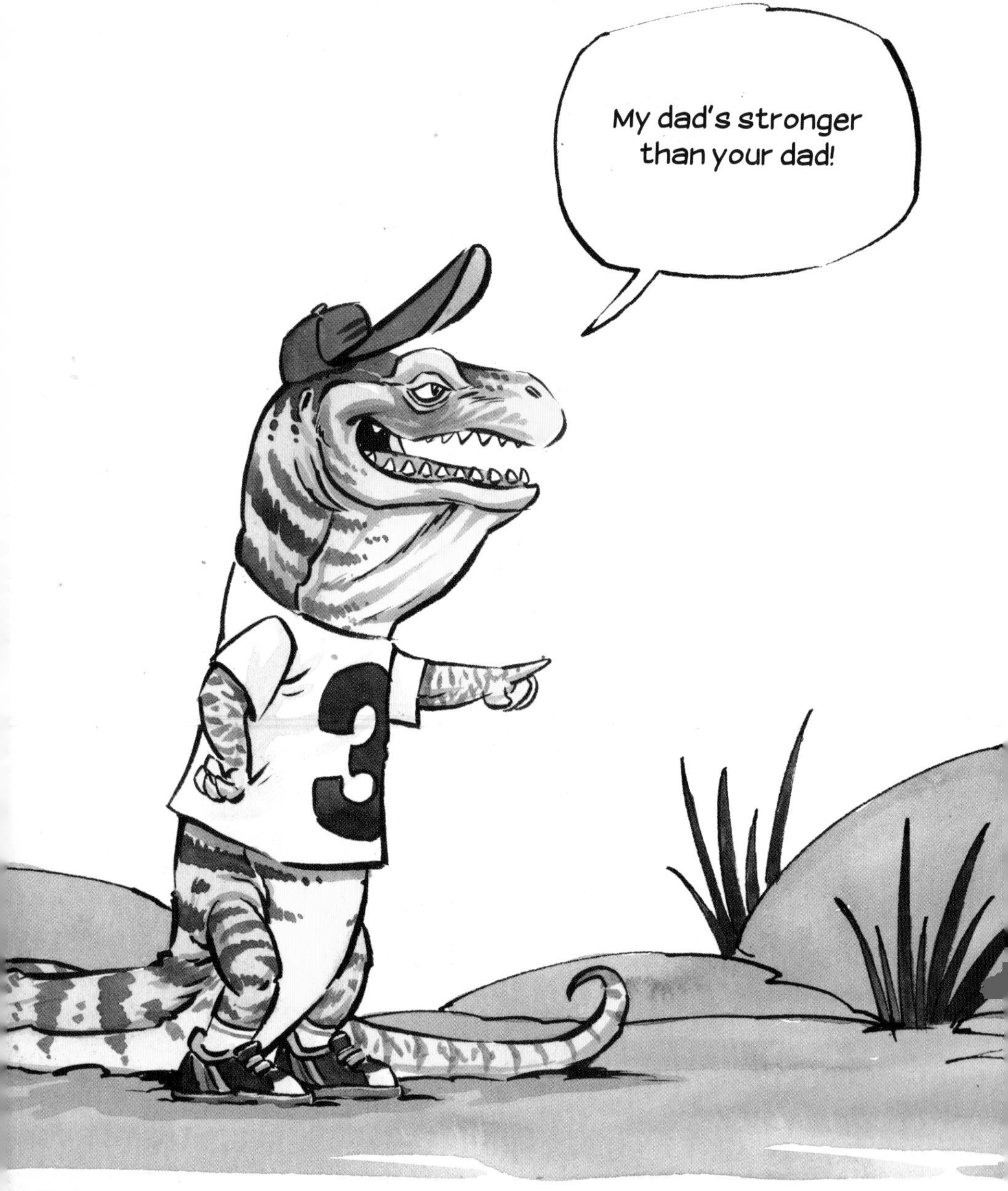
My dad's stronger than your dad!

Parthenogenesis, the process of reproduction without a mate, is a rare phenomenon in **vertebrates**. It occurs only in 0.1% of **species**. During parthenogenesis, the female can only produce male offspring.

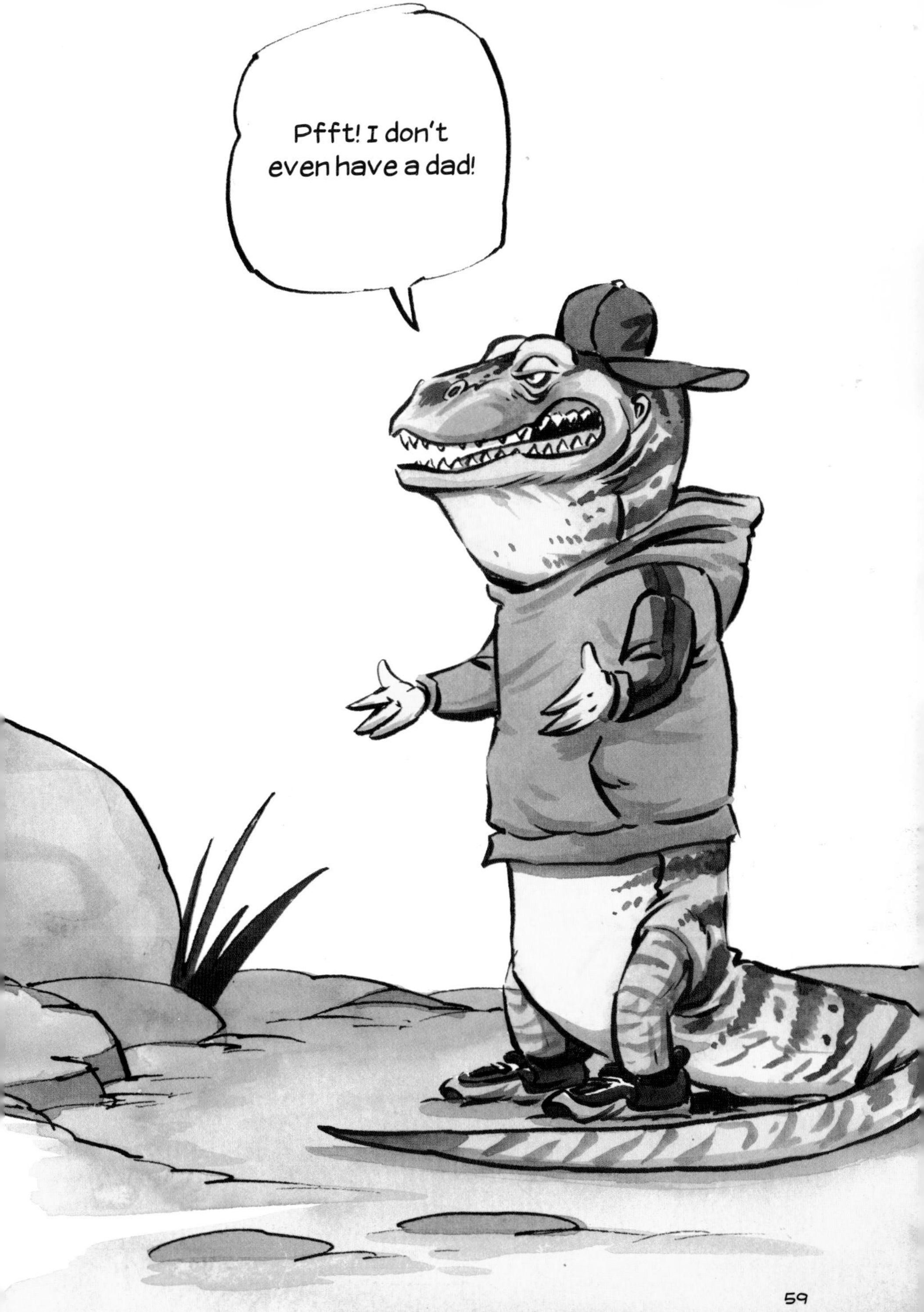
Pfft! I don't
even have a dad!

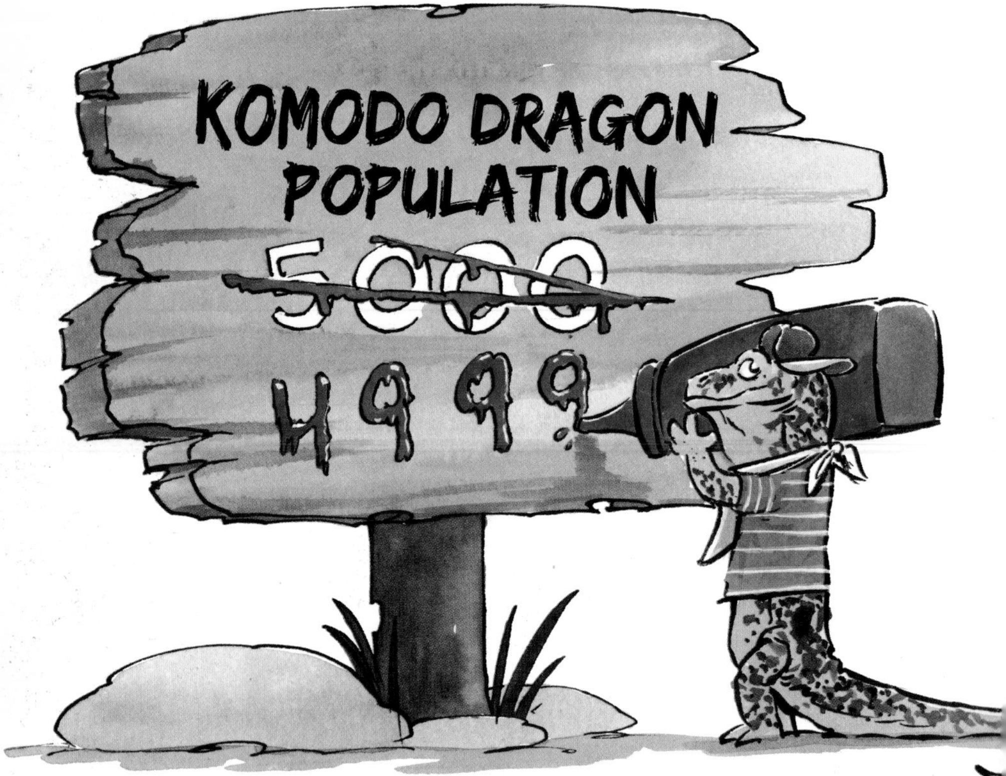
KOMODO DRAGON
POPULATION
5000
4999

The Komodo dragon is a protected species. Only 5,000 individuals exist in the world.

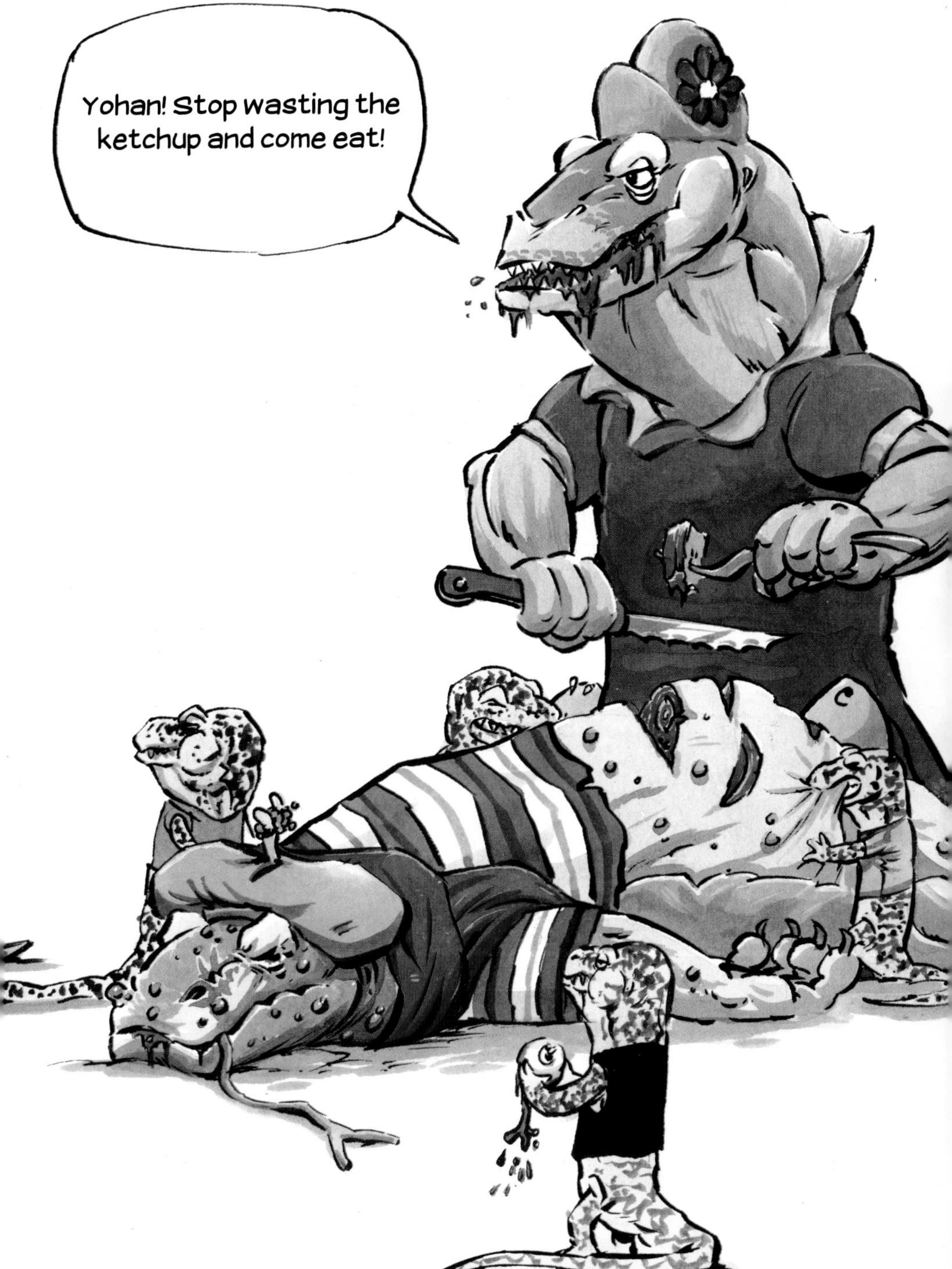
Yohan! Stop wasting the ketchup and come eat!

Glossary

Cannibal an animal that feeds on its own species

Carnivore a meat-eater

Cremate to reduce a dead body to ash by burning

Mammal a warm-blooded, back-boned animal

Predator a hunter that kills prey for food

Prey an animal hunted and killed by another for food

Reptile a cold-blooded, back-boned animal covered in scales or hard parts, such as a snake, lizard or crocodilian

Scavenger an animal that eats dead or decaying matter

Solitary living alone

Species a classification for a group of creatures with common characteristics

Territorial an animal defending its territory

Index

Do You Know there are other titles?

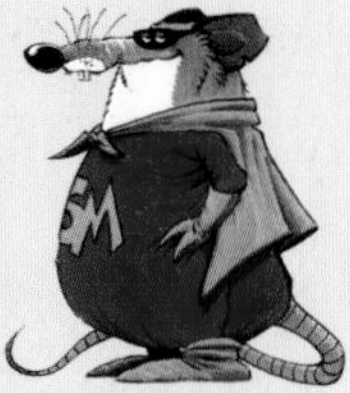
Rats

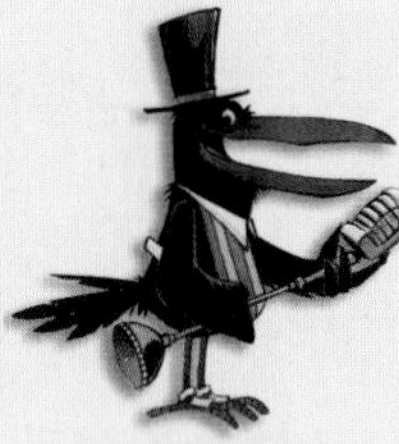
Crows

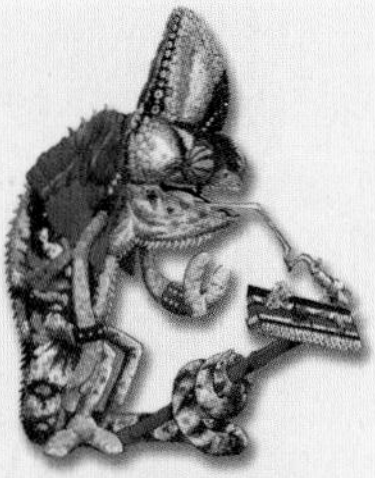
Chameleons

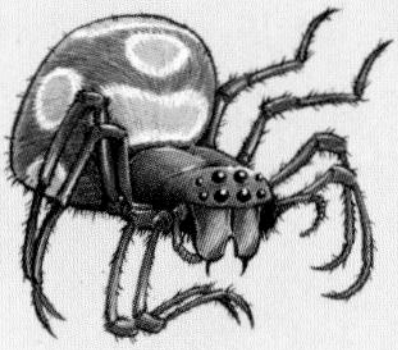
Spiders

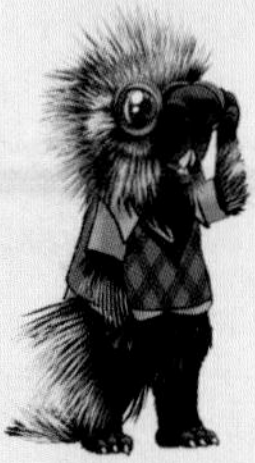
Porcupines

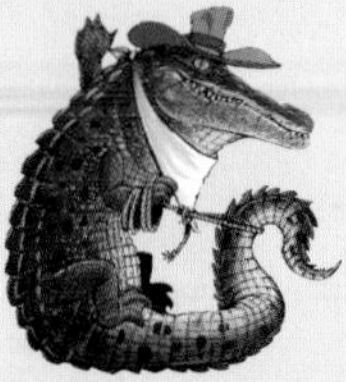
Crocodiles

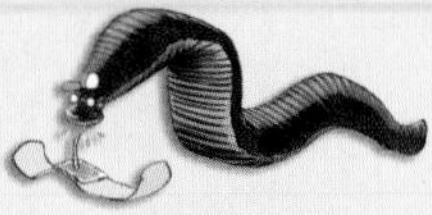
Leeches

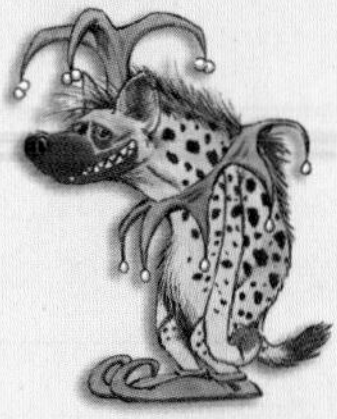
Hyenas

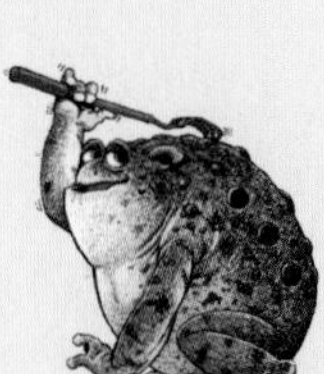
Toads

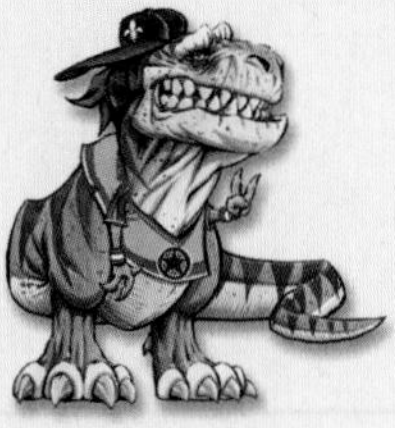
Dinosaurs

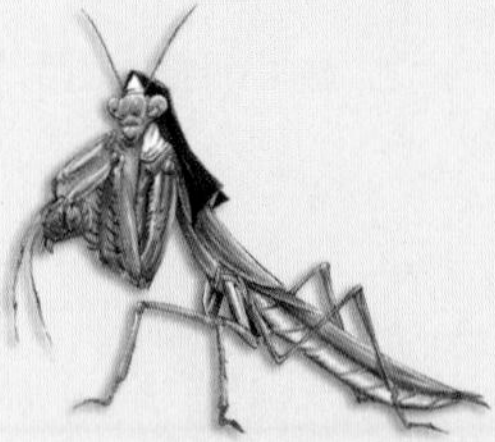
Praying Mantises